Adventures in Clowning

The Best and Worst
of the Best Times

Volume I

Compiled by Leslie Ann Akin

Global Touch Press
Lake Oswego, Oregon

Global Touch Press
Lake Oswego, Oregon

ISBN: 978-1-7327776-1-3
Printed in the United States of America

Acknowledgments

Dena Piraino, you're my right arm for proofing, editing, and publishing. Your friendship and unwavering support made this book project manageable and enjoyable.

To Jan Bear for friendship and brilliant book interior. You make it look easy.

The world is a better place for the clowns who contributed their heartfelt and heartbreaking experiences while they were in clown character. Stepping up when the opportunity appears is the hallmark of compelling leaders and these clowns are notable for their courage. You're a significant inspiration not only to fellow clowns but to people fascinated with this colorful world of bringing joy and laughter wherever you go.

Finally, to the people who helped me to this point. To my dear husband Ron Akin, who kept me nourished with his support and good cooking while I worked on the book, I'm grateful. To Cathy Gibbons, (former editor of *Laugh Makers Magazine*) who saw something in me I didn't see in myself, thank you for your trust and mentorship.

Introduction

Why this book? you might ask. Here is how *Adventures in Clowning, the Best and Worst of the Best Times,* came about. In November of 2017 I published *A Fool's Guide to Clowning.* It was long overdue. For over 25 years, I promised myself I'd write it.

I was out of the clown world for a long time, although my spirit and clown personality never left the spontaneous and wacky world of clowns. I used every tool I learned as a clown to guide me through the normal business world. As a clown, I honed my instincts, how to read people and how to juggle many situations. As a radio deejay for 12 years and graphic designer/brand specialist since 1990, I used everything I accomplished in clowning, including my sense of humor, to set myself apart from all the other folks in the business.

The success I experienced in other parts of my life were all due to valuable life lessons learned by clowning.

On December 8, 2017, I created what I expected to be a "little Facebook clown group." I reconnected with old clown friends and formed new clown friendships on-line. Many clowns wanted to take a deeper dive into the world of character development and interact about all aspects of clowning: business interactions, book-ings, creating new and funny bits of business, advanc-ing from party clowns to fairs and stage shows, and so much more.

I asked the group, "What was your most challenging experience in clowning?" The heartbreaking entries poured in. Responses were so profound that it occurred to me that I could create a book for other clowns, per-haps those who had not known they might struggle with what to do in difficult situations. We always want to stay in character, so when something troublesome happens, it's good to know how other clowns handle unforeseen problems.

Then I realized that a complete book of clowns experi-encing struggles might not be the most appealing book. So I asked the group, "What are your most gratifying experiences?" Heartwarming replies poured in. Several echoed that their times as hospital clowns and fond memories from other clowns are hysterically funny.

That's when a press release was in order—a worldwide call for entries for clowns to submit their experiences—both gratifying and challenging.

There are many delightful surprises this year. So much for thinking I was starting *"a little clown group"* on Facebook.

Thirty-two chapters in Volume I. Enjoy.

Welcome to our Facebook group:
https://www.facebook.com/groups/AFoolsGuideToClowning/

Contents

Chapter 1
Michael 'Buster' Bednarek

What I Learned One Summer

 A few summers ago, I entered the world of full-time, Big Boy Clowning after 33 years as a part-time clown, juggled with my full-time career in public education. Did I ever get schooled that summer!

With a full calendar of summer reading program shows in front of me, I spent months preparing, working out and getting in shape, scripting, routining, and rehearsing. I wanted to make the most of this opportunity. Nice plan, but it didn't factor in a little health blip that spring.

An irregular heartbeat led to a pacemaker implant and a four-week recovery period. The good news was that the heart itself was strong; it had a misfiring electrical system. Some catch-up in conditioning—extra time on the bike and in the garage studio space—got the rehearsal schedule back on track. Physically, I felt better than ever. But I was still learning lesson one:

1. There are routine, rigor, and play to good rehearsal.

I do physical comedy. I work hard while performing and demand a lot of myself physically. At my age, though, I was discovering the body didn't stretch, flex, or heal like it did years ago. In preparing to perform a busy slate of shows that summer, I had to get in shape to meet not just the physical demands, but also the performance demands.

Focus and performance-level intensity became the standard during each rehearsal to prepare for those summer shows, injected with a healthy dose of play, curiosity, and discovery.

I learned to practice how you play, as they say in the sports world. By July 1, I was ready. Then, right before my first show, I learned lesson two.

2. Be prepared and assume nothing.

I'm a list maker. I'm organized and generally leave nothing to chance. To-do lists, shopping lists, trip packing lists, Netflix lists. For my summer shows, I had a bits-and-props master list, a show order list, and a stage set-up list.

But 10 minutes before my first show, I realized that I'd forgotten to pack a very important prop, my *How to Be a Clown,* the book used at the beginning of the show! Freak! Lucky for me, I was in a library, so if you forget a prop in a library, make sure it's a book. Five minutes later, after a quick forage through the children's section, a teen volunteer came back with an armful of books. I even had choices. Whew. Clown butt saved.

Each show that summer meant a long drive from home. Forget something and don't realize it until you're setting up? There's no turning back. Either improvise, drop the bit, or sub in a backup routine. I added a detailed, itemized packing list to the pre-show routine to make sure I did not forget a prop again.

But, even packing lists aren't foolproof (fool . . . clown . . . get it?) if you assume you've got it burned in the memory banks but don't check things off. "When you assume, you . . ." I'm sure you've heard that one before. Later that summer, I fell victim to my packing assumptions again when I realized, 30 minutes before show time, that my newspaper prop was back at home on the worktable.

Lucky for me (again) I was in a library, where there are newspapers and all kinds of creative arts materials in the backroom. A handful of helpful library staff, some fast-acting and improvised prop construction, and 20 minutes later, that clown bacon was pulled from the fire, the show went on to gales of laughter, and I gave thanks for the grace that made it possible.

I learned a few additional things not to assume that summer:

1. GPS directions can sometimes lead you into dead ends on the wrong side of a park (so allow extra time).

2. Traffic volume can vary at different times of the day, especially in large metropolitan areas, wreaking havoc on estimated driving times and best routes (so allow extra time).

3. Smartphones do not know when to put themselves into airplane mode. An incoming call halfway through one show reminded me of that (so make sure it's on your stage set-up check-off list).

There were several more lessons I learned that summer:

1. Take the audience on a guided journey.
2. Know the show.
3. Listen to the audience.
4. Know the venue.
5. Learn from every performance.
6. Have a support system.
7. There is no off-season, just different seasons.

So now you know how Buster went to performing arts reality school one summer and got schooled. What can top that Summer School of Clown Knocks? That's being determined. Whatever it is, I'll play with it.

Mike "Buster" Bednarek tours throughout the Pacific Northwest with his zany mix of physical comedy, balance, and illusions called Buster's Red Nose Revue. He's served on the staff at Clown Camp™ at the University of Wisconsin–LaCrosse, Comedifest, NW Festival of Clowns, and Clowns of America International (COAI) regional and international conventions.

Mike also is the creator of Red Nose Festival Competition (http:// www.bustertheclown.net/red-nose-festival-competition.html), or simply Red Nose, which helps participants become better, more complete clowns through performance showcases and constructive critiques that focus on their strengths and areas suggested for improvement.

Now retired from a 34-year career in Oregon schools, he's trying to decide what to do when he grows up. Or, if he even wants to grow up at all. He is blessed with a loving, flexible, and forgiving wife, three daughters, three grandchildren, and a red nose. In his spare time, he cycles without falling (very often), squeezes the concertina unmercifully, and gets taken for frequent walks by his dogs.

Website: *http://bustertheclown.net*
Facebook: *https://facebook.com/BustertheClown*

Chapter 2
Scott Burkey

Adventures of a
Hospital Clown

 A recent patient really liked my sense of humor. When I told him I am a clown (and showed him my picture), you would have thought I was telling a kid that I was Santa Claus! Before he got transferred out of my unit, I signed one of my pictures and gave it to him. I literally thought he was going to cry. He acted like I had just given him a million dollars. Sadly, he passed away at home a few weeks after leaving the hospital. Knowing that I made the end of his life (but not knowing at the time), and his wife's life, a bit happier really brings joy to my heart. I will never forget him.

Tim is one of my patients I got to know well over his nine-month stay in the hospital. He finally got a heart transplant a month ago. I "clowned" around with him and his wife during their stay, and it certainly helped them during tough times. They both said I reminded them of Red Skelton and Patch Adams. I have a picture, taken the day he finally left the ICU, that represents a step on his way home!

I recently had another patient, an elderly female who was deaf. Evidently, she had some problems at another hospital because her family was very protective of her. I don't know sign language, but through my clowning and pantomime, I was able to communicate with her and literally make her laugh, which even surprised her family.

I'm really good at improv, so I just took what the situation gave me and went with it. Her family are big Ohio State fans and had her covered up with an OSU blanket.

Well, the University of Michigan–Ohio State rivalry is perhaps the biggest in college sports. So I just kept joking that I was going to make her blanket disappear, etc. Her family was playing a card game with her, too, and she indicated that one of them was looking at her cards and cheating. So I got one of our sleep masks that we have for patients and gave it to the cheater. Had the whole family laughing. When she left, the patient *told* me that I was her favorite!

Residing in Monroe, Michigan, Scott has been bringing humor to the world through clowning and magic off and on since the mid 1980s. Some of his greatest comedic influences are Red Skelton, The Three Stooges, Emmett Kelly (both Senior and Junior), Lou Jacobs, Patch Adams, Randy Christensen, and Rowan Atkinson.

He truly believes that "Laughter is the best medicine" and would love to one day start a hospital clown program!

Chapter 3
Donald 'Oddball' Carpenter

The Power of Laughter

 Forty years ago, when I was 14 years old, I had just become a professional clown.

I was with the local Clowns of America (COA later became Clowns of American International, COAI), Alley #107, at a local hospital. We had done a few skits and entertained those who were ambulatory.

Afterward, we all split up and went to various floors and wings to entertain those who were not ambulatory. I had walked into this gentleman's room and was having fun entertaining him with my puppet and some jokes.

What happened next, happened in about two to three minutes. The nurses came rushing in, and one of them asked me to wait outside the room. I waited outside the room as she asked.

The nurse came out after a couple of minutes and told me that I didn't do anything wrong. They have had several performers go into his room in the past, and the gentleman never reacted. They said I had him laughing so hard that they had to get his heart rate down.

A short time later, I was at the hospital visiting someone and thought I would check on the gentleman who I made laugh so hard. When I got to his room, it was unoccupied. I asked the nurse about him, and she said she couldn't provide any information because I was not family.

After I explained why I was asking (I was not in clown garb) she pulled me aside, it was the same nurse who pulled me out of the room. She explained that shortly after my visiting him, he made a full recovery, and they sent home him.

I'll never forget the feeling I had when I realized the power of laughter, which is why I still clown to this very day.

I was hired to entertain the children at a wedding reception while the adults enjoyed the festivities. It turns out that the children were hyper, and I swear had just been given a pound of sugar each.

Trying to keep the children entertained with some magic and balloon animals was a challenge that I hope never to repeat.

The training and knowledge I received from various conventions and lectures sure came in handy.

I am dedicated to the art of entertainment. I started magic when I was nine years old and started clowning when I was eleven years old.

At the age of thirteen, I met Hal "Shorty" Horton, a professional clown with accolades such as International Clown of The year, National Clown for the Leukemia Society, and much more. Hal took me on as an apprentice and he taught me the art of clowning, including how to properly apply my makeup, slapstick comedy, how to properly approach children, and the use of props.

Over the years I became involved with the Lucille Ball Community Theater in Jamestown, New York, where I assisted in audio/visual and set construction.

I was also a stage hand, actor, and prop handler. I was also a magic consultant for the production of Damn Yankees *at the Hartford Stage Company, in Hartford, Connecticut.*

Although I never stopped performing, I reopened my entertainment business in 2015, and I now apply my talents to enhancing events while making them fun and memorable.

In March 2018 I was elected to the position of the American South East Regional Director for the World Clown Association.

Supporting, promoting the art of clowning, and spreading joy and laughter, using any one of my talents, has been my passion since I was fourteen years old.

Website: https://musicmagicandmayhem.com/

Chapter 4
James 'Donuts D. Clown' Donoughe

It's against the Law!

My best and worst days as a working clown are probably the same days, worst when they happened, best when I look back on them.

I clowned at a community event and made the front page in full color in the local paper with my spring puppet Rocky the Racoon. Kids in the picture stood in front of my backdrop wearing the balloons. I was over the moon ecstatic at how great this was. What I didn't know was that while I was working at another event, my house was being visited and my phone was being called. Great news, the phone is ringing off the wall.

I get home to find a ton of messages Humane Society, the D.E.C, Fish and Wild Life, Dept. of Health, you name it. They called and visited my home. They interviewed my neighborhood kids asking about Rocky! They got an earful from the kids. Yeah, Donuts has a skunk, 2 chickens, a white fox, a red fox, a Rat, 2 rabbits, and a raccoon named Rocky! Then the officials asked where I keep the animals.

The city officials looked for my cages outside but there aren't any. The neighborhood kiddos, with great enthusiasm, said I keep them all in the house! This hurt! I could reach some offices and explain the confusion.

While dealing with all this, I was sitting on the porch between calls, a lady from an agency that now escapes me flashed a badge. She pulled up and yells at me. "Are you the clown in the paper?!"

I couldn't even answer as she was spewing fire and brimstone demanding to see my raccoon and the others. Saying things like, "Don't you know how dangerous it is to keep these wild animals?! They could have rabies!"

I said, "Okay, I'll bring out Rocky. Just give me a moment." I went into the house and came back to her car, where she was still spewing venom.

I played with Rocky to the fullest (my puppet. Remember, he's a puppet). She yelled at me, "You can't have a live raccoon in the city limits!"

I took Rocky and slammed him on the hood of her car and held him by the tail and said "He's *dead now*! Now can I keep him?

Her mouth about hit the floor! It was the first time she stopped yelling at me.

I explained, "It's just a puppet. They all are."

If she had asked instead of yelling at me, I would have explained it. I had to get a word in. She apologized and left. Now I make sure any reporters and their cameraman know Rocky is a puppet. That's where they all got the info from—the photographer who said, "They looked real to me." Lesson learned!

Looking for the Other Clowns

My other experience was when I was on my way to another show. Let me set the scene. It was fall, and I was driving my 1982 Toyota, a little brown beauty.

My bumper, or at least the foam under the plastic, caught fire. A few guys saw my bumper burning and were beeping and yelling for me to pull over telling me of the fire. I pulled over and got out of the car. The guys had followed to help me out until I removed my hoodie and they saw me in full clown. I kicked the bumper, and the foam came out. I stomped out the flames in my size 21 Converse leather high tops. I stomped until the fire was out.

I turned to the four guys sitting on the hood of their car laughing. I asked them, "Why didn't you help me?"

Without skipping a beat, they all stopped laughing, and one guy said, "We were waiting for your sixteen friends to get out of the car and help!" Again, they fell into hysterical laughter. I was not amused.

Looking back, this situation must have been hilarious to see! Thank the lucky stars that cell phone video wasn't a thing yet, or the incident would be viral by now. I made it to my show on time and home safe. I had to find a new car. I loved that little car.

I've been clowning for more than 30 years, I belong to WCA, Clowns of American International (COAI), and my local Alley Niagara Clown Alley. As a clown I've been able to pay my way through college, worked in two countries, clowned at parties, hotels, schools, nursing homes, local circus, street performing, you name it. I love to share what lessons I have learned on my journeys throughout my clown life.

Facebook: *https://www.facebook.com/DonutsDClown*

Chapter 5
Kimberley Anne
'Anniebelle the Clown' Eve

Affordable Fun at the Fair

 I have had many amazing experiences as a clown, but the most gratifying one was one of the first.

During one of my first walkarounds at a fair in Portland, Oregon, it did not take me long to realize how expensive the cost was for the rides, the food, the games, the souvenirs, not to mention the admission to get even a small family into the fair.

I realized the impact of these costs when many of the small families around me in the park were eating homemade sandwiches, not the fancy hot dogs, cotton candy, or elephant ears. They were drinking from juice boxes or water bottles brought from home, not slushies or sodas from the vendor booths. They were also not riding the rides that cost in some cases, five tickets or more per child per ride.

These kids were strolling through the park with big hopeful eyes, wishing they could have the fancy food other kids were eating, play the expensive runway games, and ride the fun, fast, amazing rides. Mom and Dad could not afford this for multiple kids. For many, it was all they could do to get the family in the gate and maybe, maybe, enough tickets to afford one ride per child. This is when I realized that, as a new clown, I could make a positive experience for these families.

These families did not have to pay for me. They did not have to pay for my smile or my stickers or my bubbles or my time. All it would cost me was a few minutes playing with these kids and sharing the new-found joy I had as a clown. I could take a few minutes and make them smile and make them forget, even if only for a little while, that they were eating PB&J from home instead of an elephant ear.

If they had one good memory of going to the fair, I hoped it was of the funny clown who stopped to say hello and blow bubbles with them or give them a sticker they could take home to remind them of their day at the fair.

This is when I knew I would be a clown forever. Thank you to Angel, who took a chance on me.

Kimberley Anne Eve was born in Southern California in 1960 and raised in the mountains of Big Bear Lake, California. She has also lived in Oregon, Bermuda, Georgia, Michigan, and now Colorado. Kimberley has four sons, four stepchildren, seven grandchildren and one great-grandson. Anniebelle began her clowning journey in 2012 with Angel Ocasio in Portland, Oregon. Kimberley says she is blessed and cannot believe it took her so long to find this passion.

Email: *jesseisahorse@gmail.com*

Chapter 6
Nicolas 'Scraps' Gatrell

The Value of the Unimaginable Screwup

If there's one thing that the repetitive "trial and error" approach has taught me in the realm of clowning, it's that there are not many things that count for mistakes, mishaps, or bad moments.

Everything is an equal learning experience . . . Successes, small victories, and failures. They're all lump-summed into a patchwork of moments that define how and who you are as a clown. The same way life experiences mold your character as an individual as you grow and mature. There's a connection between your personal growth and clown growth.

With that said, my own experiences haven't exactly all been perfect. Bear in mind I started at the age of 13 without any sort of mentor or teacher figure to guide me by the hand through the do's and don'ts of being an entertainer. I went out, did whatever came to my mind, and let the audience decide if it was hit or miss.

To this day, I decide what comedy material I use in my act, whether it stays or goes, using that exact method. I believe there's nothing that will tell you what you're doing is right quite the way the natural response of laughter will.

With that said, let me dig into my memory and share (one of) my biggest (absolutely awful) learning experiences.

I was around 17 years old when I first learned that sometimes there just isn't anything you can do to fix a bad audience. I'll say first that the experience wasn't entirely bad; there were good moments.

It was a birthday party for some people at my mother's job, and the event was being held at the workplace. I can still remember being self-conscious about going into a group of my mom's co-workers and entertaining. It felt, for lack of a better word, funny.

Upon arriving, I stepped out of the car, making my way to the company doors with my bouquet of 12 rainbow-pattern balloons. I took a deep breath in, deep breath out, and went inside. What ensued shortly after was nothing shy of a clown's nightmare.

To this day I wonder if by accident I had stepped into a funeral procession. These people, about twelve in all, with three kids, were in no way entertained by me or my presence. I was greeted by the stone faces of the adults in the room, and by the screeching of a child, who I didn't know was scared of balloons and (you guessed it) clowns.

Knowing I was being paid to be here, my mind commanded me to do one thing only: Work. I spent what seemed like an eternity trying my damnedest to get so much as a smile from the brick wall that was my captive audience.

There was a moment when I picked up a machine-operating manual (not knowing it was very expensive) from a shelf and dropped it on my foot in some vain attempt to break the silence. Only resulting in more indifference and possible heated anger.

After a certain amount of time, I forfeited my efforts and accepted what was a grueling defeat. I will add that later in the day, two of the kids came around and decided I was "cool." They made the blow of having just died a horrible death a bit softer.

I took away an important lesson. It was tough to process for the longest time. Being only 17 and a solo clown, the sting of being rejected by an audience was a tough one to deal with—something I didn't have much experience with either.

When you clown, you're vulnerable. You're opening a very honest part of yourself to the world and hoping for love and acceptance in return, no matter how goofy what you're doing seems. It is an extension of self, and rejection can be taken personally as I've experienced.

My lesson was that there are two kinds of people: clown people and non-clown people. In the same way we learn in normal life that there are those you can and simply cannot please, no matter the depth of effort put forth. There are moments, and lots of them, when you throw in the towel and give in, take what you can salvage, and call it a day.

The promise of something better keeps us moving and looking forward. Always another audience, always another performance, always another chance. It's one bad performance, not a bad career.

My advice to someone else who may be wondering: Never be afraid to absolutely, unimaginably, screw up. There's a golden moment of self-reflection and invaluable learning experience nestled deep in the wreckage of your pride that will teach you in a way only failure will.

Mistakes are the building blocks of creation and improvement. Build up slowly, sturdily, and carefully.

Email: *scrapstheclown@yahoo.com*

Chapter 7
Gerry 'Captain Visual' Giovinco

Quick Reaction on Stage

I was doing a performance one afternoon at a public library with a full house, mostly younger children and their parents, a typical audience for a clown magic show.

At one point, I selected a young girl out of the audience to be a volunteer and brought her up to the stage.

In the audience was a large teen-aged boy with Down syndrome who suddenly became agitated. I'm not sure if he thought I was going to hurt the little girl or what, but his disposition clearly showed that something angered him, and he lumbered to the stage on a mission! I could hear the mothers in the audience gasp as he stormed forward.

Without skipping a beat, I welcomed the boy onto the stage and immediately asked his name and introduced him to the audience just like I had introduced the little girl.

I explained that we were going to do a magic trick and asked if he wanted to help. He agreed, and though he was not sure what he got himself into, he began to relish the attention he was getting now that he was an integral part of the act!

The young man and the little girl helped me to execute my comedic magic routine that involved nesting wands, magic scarves, a change bag and a great deal of hijinks.

Both were proud of their accomplishments and exited the stage to thunderous applause but I'll never forget the glow on that boy's face when he realized that he had just become a star. A potentially scary situation was defused. A memorable moment had been created for all involved.

At the end of the show, mesmerized parents greeted me praising how I handled the situation. I told them I began my clown career as a street performer. Sometimes I feel like I have seen it all, and I acknowledged there is very little that will surprise me, a selling point I have used more times than I can remember.

Gerry Giovinco is best known for performing since 1980 as Captain Visual, the World's One and Only Super Clown. He has created several balloon books and videos that have introduced many to the great creative potential of balloon art. Beyond balloons, he is also the innovator of the PLHummer Kazoo. He is also a caricaturist that has illustrated innumerable creative coloring pages as promotional tools for clowns and entertainers everywhere!

Website: *https://captainvisual.wordpress.com/charicatures/*

Chapter 8
Hal 'Halaloo' Grant

What We Do Matters

 A teacher of my youngest asked me if I could come entertain at her un-birthday party. This was a teacher from a school where I teach balloons and juggling.

She picked a random day and invited neighbors and friends to celebrate everyone's un-birthday.

I did my normal act.

This lady had her nieces there. One was named Christina, and I spent time with her teaching her to juggle.

I had heard from Ms. Franko that her niece was heading to Vietnam on a mission trip. I thought this was terrific and thought little about it.

Ms. Franko was one of two teachers who always came out to juggling club to learn. After club one day, I was telling Ms. Franko about the impact she had on our son. How thankful he had been in her grade-one class. Then she said, "The impact you have with all you do, not just here but well beyond your reach." She then said she wanted to send me an email her niece had sent.

This is the email I received:

> Hi Hal, Here is what my niece just sent me from Vietnam.
>
> > Hi there!
> >
> > It's Christina. :)
> >
> > I had the most amazing time in Vietnam, and one of my favorite memories was teaching (well trying to teach) this one little boy and his sister how to juggle. They thought it was the coolest thing ever!
> >
> > I was just wondering if you could pass this pic along to the clown who taught me how at your un-birthday party a couple summers

ago. I'm so grateful he taught me how cuz I can't believe how many smiles it got. :)

Hal, this is just one story. I am certain there are many more that you will never hear. I want you to know what YOU DO makes a difference! Not just in the lives you come directly in contact with, but also in the lives of who they come in contact with. Through you sharing your gift with my niece at my un-birthday party, you brought smiles to the young boy (in the photo) and his sister. But also, to the many others that were part of the mission team there with Christina. We are blessed to have you give so much time to us at St. Martins. Thank you,

Ms. Franko.

I share this as a reminder to all clowns. Every event you do may have moments that seem insignificant to you, but mean so much to those you are entertaining. And what's more, the impact you may have is far beyond the *ring* in which you perform.

My take away: No moment you give of yourself is a small moment.

The Birthday Party
from H E Double Toothpicks!

I received a call about a birthday party from an agent. After I held firm to my rate, he finally agreed and booked me for the event.

The day arrived, and I set out for the party. It started out rough, because I couldn't find the home. I learned that a farm field had split the road, and I finally find the location.

I arrived, the house was small. There were no trees, and a hay field that had been recently cut surrounded the house. Great for when I started doing balloons. There was going to be plenty of popping going on. The driveway was packed with cars. There were at least twenty cars parked in a long driveway. I parked at the end because I wanted a fast getaway!

Many of the adults had been drinking most of the afternoon. There was a bouncy castle in the back yard.

I set up as I normally do. Setting up is part of my act. My show was off and running (it should have been me running—running away!). There were more than 24 children at this birthday party. They had told me there would be 12.

I do a comedy magic show and balloons. Halfway through the show, the person who owned the bouncy castle came to take it down. There were children still on it, three or four by now. Others were focused on me. The few left on the castle would not get off. Then it turned into a game, and more got on the bouncy castle.

Guess what the person there to take it down did? He pulled the plug from the generator and let the air out while the children were still bouncing. Only two parents tried to get the children off.

I stepped out of character for a moment and told the parents that were sitting with the children that the bouncy castle was not part of my services. The kids were still trying to bounce as the castle was deflating. It was not quick enough for the guy taking it down, so he found a place where it had been patched with duct tape. He tore the tape off to finish the job! Again, I stepped out of character and said I was in no way connected to the people providing the bouncy castle. A couple of moms motioned for me to continue my show. I did!

Leaving, I thought, "Never again." "This is it!" It was bad. Two moms at the party thanked me for soldiering on. They wanted to hire me for their children's birthday parties. And they did for other events too.

The entire time I kept thinking, "Is it time to go?" "How bad can this get?" "I am not doing my best."

I learned that you are never as bad as you think you were. And remember to *always* ask the right questions at the time you take the booking! Have a telephone interview when answering all inquiries.

Hal "Halaloo" Grant has been clowning for more than 23 years and has portrayed Santa almost as long. He has written for many clown magazines and has taught at conventions and led workshops. Currently he oversees Clowns of America International online Alley (Alley 1000)

His first love is clown ministry. It has allowed him to clown in Canada and the USA. He has also clowned overseas in Nicaragua and the Philippines. He lives in Ontario, Canada, with his family

Website*: http://www.halaloo.ca/*

Chapter 9
Deanna 'Dee Dee' Hartmier

Cheering the Broken-Hearted

I had always heard of other clowns who have had this happen, but until Mumbai in 2015 I had never experienced it. Jameelah means "beautiful" in Arabic. I think we all had trouble saying the girl's name, so we called her Jameelah. Her family was from Yemen.

The group of clowns did a show at the Tata Memorial Hospital. The children had a coloring contest ,and the winning artwork was presented to us, then given to me. It was a beautiful memory. The artwork is hanging in my clown room at home.

Then we were asked to go to a couple of wards to visit children who could not leave their rooms. This was the cancer ward. We entered a room with a young girl about thirteen to fifteen years old who had been non-responsive for two months due to her pain. We talked with her and her parents.

As I do little hospital clowning, I took classes from Patty Wooten. I always try to get knowledge from every area of clowning, just because you never know when you might need it. Remembering some skills she taught, I started doing them with this young girl. I was holding her left hand, breathing with her. Her eyes moved. I wasn't sure if I saw correctly. I continued holding her hand and even sang a song softly. Next, she smiled. None of us could believe what we saw. Her parents were so joyful to see their daughter respond. We were elated with joy.

Then it was time to leave. I was the last to leave the room, and Jameelah actually waved. It was so difficult not to cry with joy at what just happened.

What an amazing feeling knowing you touched some-one in such a way to bring her out of her pain even if it was for a few moments. She touched all of us. This young girl who had been nonresponsive for two months. Our caring and spending time with her made a huge impact for this young girl and her family.

Two days later her father brought her to our show at the mall. She walked onto the stage for pictures, and I received a hug! Words cannot express the feeling when you know what you are doing is so worthwhile.

Lifting the Spirit

One day after clowning for several hours, I was walking out of a mall with my arms and hands full of my supplies. A woman with a disorder saw me.

She cried out, "Dee Dee!" and ran toward me. I knew she wanted a hug, so I put my stuff down and prepared for the embrace. Little did I know what would happen next.

While Elsie was hugging me, she said she just came from the doctors. "Oh, Dee Dee, I've had such a bad day. A bad man broke into my home and raped me."

I felt my heart jump into my throat. I didn't know what to say or do, allowing her to tell me her story. I told her she was special, and no one should be afraid in their own home. I made her a balloon. Then we all, Elsie, her family, and I, said our farewells.

I picked up my stuff and just felt drained and horrible about what happened to Elsie. When I got to my car I cried.

Two weeks later, a few ladies came into my normal job and said they knew what I did. I was confused because

I didn't know what they were talking about. Then they told me two weeks earlier they happened to be at a restaurant. A young woman was showing everyone the balloon I gave her and telling them I told her she was special. They had heard this story. I changed and helped lift Elsie's spirit.

The whole point of this story is no matter where we go or what we do, we never know how or who we touch or help. Giving to people, even if it is a moment for them to forget their troubles, tells me what we do is so worthwhile. I just managed to hear and see the power we have as clowns.

Deanna Hartmier "Dee Dee the Clown" couldn't find a clown for her daughter's fifth birthday in 1995. So she jumped in with both clown feet and in 2000 married Cliff "Mister Stripes" Hartmier with a clown wedding. She was the 2015 World Clown Association (WCA) Clown of the Year and President of the WCA 2013–15. Canadian Central Director of the WCA (2007–13). Clowns Canada–Central West Ambassador

She has won several awards: Best Overall Clown for the North Dakota State Fair (2000 and 2001). The prize includes performance, paradability, and balloons. Second place for Comedy Whiteface WCA Convention Denver CO (2009. Third place for Comedy Whiteface WCA Winnipeg (2010). International Face Painting Award winner (2013)

Deanna is co-owner of Laughter Without Borders (http://www.laughterwithoutborders.com/) an entertainment agency in Winnipeg Canada. She was also instrumental in establishing LAFS Canada Inc. (http://www.lafscanada.ca/), which is a charity for teaching life and fire safety in schools around the province.

Dee Dee has taught and performed in Canada, United States, Caribbean Cruises, India (2010 and 2015), Hong Kong (2013 and 2015), Malaysia (2013 and)2015, Ireland 2015, Denmark 2016, and England 2018.

Website*: http://www.deedeetheclown.com/*

Chapter 10
Ron Jaffe

Accidentally Scary

 As new clowns, we often forget that our brightly colored makeup and exaggerated clothing amplifies the intensity of the things we say and movements we make.

In our street clothes, a diminutive wave with our fingertips says "Hello," but in clown, that same wave comes across as a loud, "Hi there! How are you!?"

I had forgotten this when a small child about two years old was wheeled up near our booth in a stroller-wheelchair. Disabled, unable to use his arms or legs, he had some kind of breathing apparatus. He didn't see me, but I was about to make his day and inadvertently set the stage for a probable lifelong fear or disgust of clowns.

Completely forgetting I had on bright facial makeup with blue hair, and completely forgetting I had on bright clothing with contrasting stripes and plaids, and completely forgetting how large I was, and completely forgetting how large my shoes were and how loud a "kapow" sound those shoes make when I slap them down onto the pavement, I jumped in front of this child's stroller with a huge smile, a loud double-kapow from my feet, a loud cheery "Howdy!" and a wide open-armed greeting.

For two full seconds, which seemed like minutes, there was no reaction.

Time stopped. I remained still, the parents remained still, the other clowns remained still and the child in the stroller remained still until— You've probably heard the term "scream like a banshee," and until that moment I did not understand what a banshee sounded like.

But after two very long seconds, I found out. That poor child let out with the most horrendously terrifying scream I had ever heard.

My goal of hearing the child's jubilant laughter disappeared as quickly as a flat screen TV on Black Friday. Instead, I knew at that moment I had probably instilled a lifelong fear of clowns into this precious child's memory.

I went into apology mode, saying all I could to the parents to let them know how bad I felt. Meanwhile, I berated myself as a moron for forgetting the effects of over-exaggerated facial features and loud, brightly colored costumes on the smallest of humans.

The parents probably felt as bad for me as I did for their child. I gave one last apologetic nod to them and backed off. Something else attracted their son's attention and for the moment at least, it seemed I was off the hook.

Over the years this lesson stuck with me and is one I share with each new class of clowns as a testament to the power of a clown's image.

I still think now and again about that child and wonder if our chance meeting had any long-term effects, but I no longer berate myself.

After all, my intentions were good. I was just careless. It was a moment of naivete, and just the thing you'd expect from a foolish clown.

A clown his whole life, with much of his childhood spent in detention for being a class clown, Ron finally connected with greasepaint in the winter of 2011 when he went through clown school at Fun World Clown Alley in Orlando, Florida.

Since that time he and his clown-wife Aracelis have continued their education while teaching other clowns and while sharing their gift of humor with at-risk children and seniors. Ron is also a professional puppeteer and actor at a local history museum and is itching to one day have a full-sized professional flea circus.

Chapter 11
Bruce 'Charlie' Johnson

Responding to Disaster

 I was the headliner for a clown ministry conference in McMinnville, Tennessee. On the morning of February 1, 2003, I was getting ready to begin my Tramp Tradition Show in which I recreate routines performed by famous or significant tramp clowns throughout history. It is a fully scripted multimedia performance with a narrator. I was stretching backstage while the conference director was finishing the morning announcements. Suddenly somebody burst in the back door to announce that the Space Shuttle Columbia had just broken up during re-entry.

For the next forty minutes, people shared their feelings and prayed. Suddenly the director said, "And now here is Charlie in the Tramp Tradition."

Without warning, I had to make my entrance. I did not complete my normal final mental preparations. I was still dealing with my own feelings of grief. I wasn't able to concentrate on what I was performing. Fortunately, I was well rehearsed and could do the first few routines on autopilot. Gradually I focused on the performance and be present. I played with the audience.

I performed Emmett Kelly's cabbage routine and wandered into the audience carrying a head of cabbage. I stared soulfully at a woman while absent-mindedly nibbling at the cabbage. Remembering my manners, I offered her the cabbage. Then I wandered off to find another woman to fall in love with. Then I offered a little of the cabbage to one woman, she grabbed the entire head. I thought, "How dare you." I shook my head. Then I thought, "Maybe she needs it more than me." I sighed and turned towards the stage. I felt everyone in the audience inhale at once, and then in unison, they all went "Ah!" I knew I had unified the audience helping them forget their grief. The rest of the show went great.

After the show, the conference director told me they had decided to cancel the rest of the conference and send everyone home. However, they changed their mind while watching my show. They felt I had demonstrated how clowning can help people deal with shock and grief. They decided that was an important lesson for the participants so they allowed the conference to continue.

A week later I received a card from a conference participant. She said she didn't know how she would cope initially with her emotions. Then she watched me as a Tramp encountering difficulties, refusing to give up, and ultimately finding success. She said my performance gave her hope.

I had a similar experience while lecturing and performing at a clown festival in England on September 11, 2001.

Those were obvious tragedies. We don't know what private personal tragedy any member of an audience may be experiencing. However, our performance can help them deal with it. This is one reason clowning is so very important.

Gratitude for Small Gifts

One of my duties while touring with Circus Kirk in 1976 was posing with customers in the Clown Photo Studio. We had a customized Polaroid camera system that timed the development process for us. The photo studio was in a tent on the circus midway. I was scheduled to start at the studio one hour before each performance.

I quickly learned that it did not work for me to sit in the studio waiting for people to come in for their photo. People were more likely to want a souvenir with me if I had established a relationship with them. So as soon as the midway opened, I entertained people waiting for the gates to open. The sideshow performance began a half hour before the main show. As soon as the sideshow started, the gates to the Big Top opened. The midway quickly emptied as people streamed inside to find their seats.

The photo studio would close. I would enter the Big Top to perform during the Come In. I concentrated on forming a connection with the audience.

As soon as the main performance ended, I dashed around behind the tents to reach the photo studio. If I was lucky, people would line up for photos. If not, I stood in front of the studio tent entertaining people hoping they would not continue out the exit.

Sometimes, when I got a family to stop, some members browsed the nearby souvenir stand and purchased something there.

The items in the souvenir stand varied in price, with a clown doll being the most expensive one.

After one performance, a preschool girl approached me on her own. She was carrying one of the clown dolls. She handed it to me. I admired it and started to hand it back to her. She said it was for me. I looked around and nobody seemed to pay attention to us. I didn't know if her parents knew she would offer the doll to me. I didn't want to take it and be accused of stealing it. I didn't think she should offer me something that expensive. I insisted that she take the doll back.

Her face immediately crumbled. I realized that when I rejected her gift, she felt I was rejecting her.

I did everything I could to cheer her up. I inflated a balloon and offered it to her. I did some little gags. Nothing worked. She was inconsolable. Finally, she sadly turned away, trudged across the midway, and left with her parents. I didn't have a chance to explain to them what had happened.

Since then I have always tried to be a gracious recipient of any gift offered no matter how big or small. I know that by accepting their gift, I am accepting them.

Chapter 12
Janice 'Groovy' Johnson

Here Comes the Parade Clown

I tried out for the Rose Festival Character Clown Corps and was offered the opportunity to join. In April, I attended a weekend workshop and went home with a huge pair of purple pants. I spent weeks shopping for the rest of my costume.

In June, I joined a group of Rose Festival clowns waiting for the Starlight Parade to begin. One clown had two huge front teeth and a hunk of hair stuck straight up through the top of her ragged hat. A beautiful dark-skinned clown wore green eyelashes and danced like an ethereal being.

When a woman asked to have a photograph taken with us, a bald clown took a new clown nose from his bag, and with exaggerated movement, placed it carefully on the nose of the requestor. She squealed with joy as we gathered around her. I loved these fun people.

The truck in front of us started its bubble machine and crept forward. As we rounded the first corner and met the crowd, I heard, "Here come the clowns!" People waved. Someone shouted, "I love you!" I waved wildly. The enthusiasm buoyed me to a place I've never been—clown nirvana.

After a few blocks of floating on air, I felt the hard pavement under my fancy feet and changed waving arms. Around me clowns juggled, rode unicycles and danced. I only knew how to wave so I stayed at the front of the group to ride the wave of initial enthusiasm.

A few blocks down, a man stopped me and said, "End of the parade." I didn't want it to end, but grudgingly turned right and started my search for a bathroom.

A week later, I headed for the Grand Floral Parade. Thirty clowns gathered in a meeting room at the Memorial Coliseum. We had two unicycle riders, one miniature bike rider and two who held signs. One demanded rights for balloon animals. My sign said, "Smiling is contagious."

As we marched out of the Coliseum, one of the unicycle riders fell and the clowns rushed over, screaming, "Is the bike okay?" They ignored the fallen man and studied the bike. Then they announced to the crowd, "The bike is okay," and walked away. After three falls, I realized it was a gag.

Photographers snapped me and my sign. The crowd yelled, "You're right." Many showed me an exaggerated grin or pointed to a sad neighbor. Someone screamed, "You're wrong. It's laughter. Laughter is contagious." He was right. My sign was wrong. I'd gotten it wrong. I felt embarrassed.

By the end of the parade my feet hurt, and I was thirsty. I followed a group of clowns to the Max station and rode home. "How'd it go?" asked my husband. I tried to explain the rush of pleasure I'd felt interacting with the crowd and didn't mention the bad part.

Private Performance

My mother had been in hospice for eight months, and I had watched her slipping away. She no longer was able to get out of bed to eat her meals. She took her baths in the bed. I had trouble deciphering her breathless whispers. In fact, she didn't even open her eyes anymore when I visited. It was painful for me to see her this way, but I continued my visits to her bedside in the adult family care home on a regular basis. I felt hopeless and helpless. There was no way to reach her.

I thought of the questions I never got a chance to ask her. Where was the soda fountain her parents owned in Spokane? Who were the relatives in Sweden she and my father visited? Why had she been so hard on me?

Even as she lay in bed, I was still scared of her. Would she blurt out another criticism of my hair? My family? My life?

As a new clown with Portland's Rose Festival I had been shy about showing her my new costume, Groovy the Hippy Clown, fearing a negative reaction. In late May I finished getting ready for the first parade of the year, the St. John's Parade. I found I had an hour to spare. In a rush of enthusiasm, I grabbed my gloves and tie-dyed shoulder bag and drove the mile to the adult care home where she lived.

I rushed through the front door, waved at the caregiver who looked flustered until she recognized me and walked into my mom's room. Her eyes flew open and followed me around the room. I waved my purple-gloved hand at her and smiled broadly, "Hi, Mom," I said, in my loudest voice. "Groovy is here to entertain you."

Her eyelids flickered ,and she may have smiled.

I twirled for her so she could see the entire costume: sparkling gold hi-tops, striped socks, patchwork pants, tie-dyed shirt, purple fringed vest and a huge blonde afro wig with a head band. I stopped and bowed. Her eyes stayed open.

My arms danced. My head bobbed. My hips swung around in a circle.

Then I pulled out Stinky, my skunk puppet, and he snuggled into her cheek. "I think Stinky likes you," I said. "Better watch out he doesn't—" I lifted Stinky's tail just enough to suggest a spray. Stinky escaped from my grasp and flew into the air. I caught him and returned him to my shoulder bag.

Next, I produced a giant feather and drew it across her cheek.

She spoke. I moved closer to hear what she was saying. "You're funnier than you think you are," she said, then closed her eyes. I gave her a light kiss on the forehead before I left. On my way out, I pondered my mother's words. I think she liked the show.

Janice Johnson has been with the Rose Festival for five years as Groovy the Hippy Clown and is a member of the Rose City Clown Alley. She clowns with her therapy dog, Mr. Morgan, who also dresses like a hippy. Together they march in the parades, visit City Fair, and volunteer at camps, banquets, street fairs and other events. She writes about sailing for adults and writes for middle-graders and teens.

Website: *https://jjkay.net/*

Chapter 13
David 'Dizzy Dave' Keenan

The Praise of Fellow Clowns

 I was at a clown convention about ten years ago. While there, I made friends with a clown who would soon become a producing clown with the RBB&B Circus. He and his acting partner stood out with their awesome makeup and costuming, they were friendly and approachable. We were lining up for a parade schtick competition, and he told me I stood out in the crowd of clowns.

That was more epic than winning an award in my book. Affirmations like this are gratifying experiences as they tell me I'm doing something right in my clown development. Being complimented both by other clowns and by the public definitely encourages me to keep going.

At a small circus, our alley went to a performance as guest clowns, doing the meet-and-greet before the show and during intermission. They seated us for the show, and the clown behind me told me that a fan pointed me out while we performed saying, "There's one good-looking clown." This from a group of clowns! Having fun in parades, and the reactions from the crowd are the most gratifying experience.

At a recent Halloween kids' parade, I donned my homemade Howdy Doody outfit, with a 'mast' attached to a rig I stitched onto the back of my outfit so that a full set of (elastic) Marionette Strings could look realistic. As our group made that first turn (every parade has that first turn from assembly area to "You're on!"), I saw all the faces turned towards me and heard the voices of surprise. Those strings might as well have been lifting me off my feet. I was so pumped.

This sort of thing happened at a Fourth of July parade. I sat in the rear of a golf cart full of clowns, facing back. The driver serpentined to give people a closer look at us as we rode by. I wore a homemade space suit, complete with air-fed plastic bubble helmet, and so many jaws dropped I could have made a mint as a facial surgeon.

Be Remembered Favorably

Back in the late 1980s, there was a lot more selfishness as far as keeping secrets and being competitive every minute of every day. A clown came back from RBB&B Clown College. I asked him if he could help me develop my make-up and costume. He told me flat-out he "doesn't want any super-clowns competing against me" even though I told him I was into parades and freebie events, not the birthday party business. He only helped another clown who became his employee and performing partner.

I got more of that at a clown convention in 1988, when people formed cliques and kept the rest of us from being able to share in the experiences of legends in attendance. There were a lot of sour faces behind greasepaint. Fortunately, I discovered that there was the Sharing Mindset that now prevails in the clowning community, but there are still the jealous cliques. My best defense mechanism is pretty much my mindset, especially at age 53. I have fun and prevail despite the haters. That's the best way to battle them. Let them do any damage and be the bad guy when out in public. This leads to my personal motto: Be Remembered Favorably.

As a kid in the 1970s, I wanted to be part of one of the 'epic' clown groups (circus or local), and as an adult, I'm trying to keep that dream alive. Clowning became a way out of social isolation with my Asperger syndrome, and I have made a lot of clown friends along the way.

Email: *chainblaster@gmail.com*
Facebook: *https://facebook.com/PlasticBubbleCosplay/*

Chapter 14
Edmund 'Captain Dazzle' Khong

Enlightened Clowning

 My clown name is Captain Bubbles. I am from the tiny country-state of Singapore, an independent country in Southeast Asia. In 2014, I attended Clown Camp Singapore where many good US and Japanese clowns, led by Dr. Richard Snowberg, performed and taught clowning. That is where I met the Japanese ladies clown duo, RONE and Gigi, Clown Camp Japan directors and chief instructors in 2015. Dr. Snowberg, the founder of Clown Camp in the United States was the special VIP instructor.

Japanese clowns take their training seriously. Their style of teaching and learning differs greatly from the West. In the West, students ask questions and clarify doubts at any juncture. In Japan, whenever the lesson has begun, there are clear distinctions between teacher and student, and both have specific roles to play. The student questions only after he or she has mastered the core training as provided by the teacher. There are pros and cons to each style.

Japanese clowns are deeply dedicated to mastering and honing their skills. One of them is Yukky, (pronounced Yoo-key) a lady clown with an earnest attitude to learning. She began clowning in 2014 at Clown Camp Japan, and I could see a big jump in her skills one year later at the 2015 Clown Camp. Just before going out to a Caring Clown visit to an elderly nursing home, I could see her putting on her makeup and costume early, so she could put in some additional practice time at her pantomime and juggling.

At the end of the Caring Clown visit, all of us returned to the classroom for a debrief. Yukky shared her experience. She said she felt useless because, throughout the visit, she did nothing because an elderly lady resident took her hand and held on to her throughout the entire 90 minutes we were there. The elderly resident only spoke to Yukky. Yukky said she felt terrible because she could see that all of us were clowning, juggling, magic and balloon sculpturing, while she did the least among all of us because she never got the chance to do her practiced clown routines.

RONE asked the fellow participants if we had anything to contribute before she gave her feedback. I injected and said Yukky did the most during the visit. She gave this elderly resident what she needed most, the human touch and a listening ear. As Caring Clowns, our focus should be on the patients we're serving. Yukky had tears in her eyes. At that moment I realized how important our words and actions are as Caring Clowns. We need to support each other because Caring Clowning requires more awareness and subtlety.

Dr. Snowberg concluded the session by reminding us that Caring Clowning comprises two words, caring and clowning, and both aspects are important. Many times, as Caring Clowns, we spend a lot of time sharpening our clowning performance skills, but we should also invest equal effort and time in learning how to care. Yukky's sharing and Dr. Snowberg's message resonated with me deeply. Ever since then, just before I embark on a Caring Clowning visit, I always recall this wonderful shared experience. It has made my Caring Clowning very meaningful and I will continue to use my skills for good for the rest of my life.

The Case of the Missing Nose

I attended Clown Camp Japan again in 2017. All of us performed a clown skit or variety act for open mic. I was scheduled to perform my clown magic act at a community club for families and children. It was a beautiful day, too, and all of us were eager to perform. We woke up at 7 a.m., had a quick breakfast, and hopped into the bus with all our equipment. I did multiple checks on all my props because I wanted to ensure I had everything I needed for the stage show.

The bus journey took us up the hills, and everything was going great until I saw my reflection in the rear mirror of the bus. I had forgotten my clown nose. My heart stopped for a few seconds. Wait, am I imagining this? I looked in the mirror again. Yup, it is not there. Where my round red latex nose would be, was just a simple and faint red dot. It was my third year at Clown Camp Japan, so I had a good idea of how some Japanese clowns would react if I announced that I had forgotten about my clown nose. It would not be good.

I calmed myself down and spoke to Sayaka, a great supporter of Clown Camp Japan. An alarmed Sayaka said, "What?! You will need the nose!" I told her to calm down, it is a small matter, that there is nothing to be concerned about. No one had noticed that I did not have my clown nose on. Her reaction was unexpected despite all my best efforts to not make a big deal.

My thoughts were, "Hey Driver, can we turn back? How much time do we have? Do we have time to turn back? What can we do?!"

I had my makeup on and assured Sayaka that everything would be fine. I asked, "If I didn't tell you, you wouldn't have noticed the missing nose, right?" Sayaka became anxious. She asked the other participants if any of them had a spare nose. No one had an extra nose. Many of them also became distressed for me. Thinking back, I am amused at their reactions, but it goes to show how dedicated the Japanese are toward their chosen craft.

Many clowns offered their own clown nose, and they said they would hide in a room and not take part in the meet-and-greet. I said no; the mistake is mine and I will bear it. I searched my pockets to see if I might have misplaced my nose. (Who else but a clown misplaces their nose?!) Nope, it was not there, but I found a red sponge ball I use for magic.

The children loved the show, and a local newspaper covered it.

The lesson here is that many times, as clown performers, we're obsessed with perfecting everything and forget about the big picture. Unexpected problems and accidents will occur occasionally. If I had allowed myself to get overly stressed over a missing clown nose, I might have fumbled during my show.

Focus on doing the best you can with what you have.

Singapore-based clown Edmund Khong loves children and making them laugh. Edmund is one of four Master Clowns recognized by the World Clown Association. Edmund is the Southeast Asia Regional Director, taking care of the WCA Alleys in his area. He is an advocate of lifelong learning and loves sharing his knowledge and skills.

Website: *https://www.captaindazzle.com/*

Chapter 15
Robert Benjamin Lawrence

Clowns and Reading

 Friday was the last day of the Read Across America week (usually celebrated as Dr. Seuss Week as well). I went to a local school on the invitation of a friend who teaches there. The school had a little parade, and I was able to clown it up and ride my mini bicycle in the parade.

Afterward I read a book to her class, a book about not being afraid of clowns. This class didn't need any help with that, though. They were awesome!

When the book was over, with a little help from the class, I was able to magically make some candy appear for all of them. They loved everything: the bike, the story, the candy, and all my shenanigans.

They loved it so much they wanted me to read a second book to them, which I happily did. This one, *This Book Has No Pictures*, I was not familiar with.

The kids loved it, and if you ever do read along to kids, I highly recommend it, it's fantastic, and gives plenty of chances to play around, even if there are no pictures.

I've known this was what I wanted to do with my life for some time, but if I hadn't already, this one experience would have sold me on it. It was magical in the truest sense of the word and left me on cloud nine for the rest of the day.

Chapter 16
Cheryl 'Tic Toc' Lekousi

Cheering the Helpless

Hearts & Noses Hospital Clown Troupe visits children's bedsides at five Boston-area hospitals. Two are medical rehabilitation pediatric units where we might see the same children for weeks, months, or even years. This has given us time to form more than casual relationships. Once we have permission to enter a child's room, we try to connect, offer play, and follow the game where ever the child's play leads us.

Stopping at the door of young Jen's room, I peeked in to let her see me. When her eyes met mine, she wept deep sobs. I immediately told the nurse I had upset this child. The nurse shared with me that eight-year-old Jen had just arrived from an acute-care hospital. "Her neck is broken. She can't move, speak, or breathe on her own. She cries whenever anyone is in sight. She's grieving her loss. You're welcome to visit her."

I spoke to my partner, Poppy. My gut feeling was for a quiet visit, offering a story or song. Poppy felt that one clown would be enough, so she stayed back, waiting to see if she should join us. Knowing Jen would cry once I was in sight, I moved slowly where she could see me. Her room was filled with Christmas decorations, dolls, and toys she couldn't hold.

I sat in the visitor's chair and asked if she would like to hear a holiday story. She stopped crying as soon as I spoke. I learned that once engaged she would focus on what was happening. That day I wanted to clown for her, offer her something of meaning, and watch for any way I could give her control.

"Would you like a holiday story?" One blink, yes. What Christmas story would Tic Toc tell? *The Big Pumpkin* by Erica Silverman felt just right (even though Christmas isn't Halloween). The pumpkin is too big for the witch to pick up to make into a pie. The ghosts and mummies, vampires, and the witch meant lots of voices and action. None of these big characters can pick up the pumpkin. Then along comes a little bat with an idea.

Jen watched while I told and acted out the story. I didn't know how it went until later when Poppy told me she saw Jen take a deep breath and relax as the bat saved the day.

Over the next eight months, Poppy and I created a girls' club with Jen. We would ask a question and make an offer. Would you like to travel today? Blinking was her only way to communicate. Yes? Her smile directed our play. Out would come our kazoos to make our motorcycle engines roar, and away we'd go.

A Clown's Persuasion

Another partner, Kow Girl Koo, and I were visiting an acute-care hospital. One nurse asked if we could help in a room. It seems four-year-old Mike was holding his medicine in his mouth and not swallowing. As we entered, we saw two nurses, a mother, and an aide all pleading with Mike to swallow. No clowns needed here with all those people saying *swallow*, but we might as well stay and play.

Koo and I removed everything from Mike's dinner tray and I took a ping-pong ball out of my bag. We asked for two straws. Ignoring Mike and his mouth full of medicine we blew the ball back and forth. This was such a fun game that Mike reached for the straws to play too. Koo stopped and said to no one in particular "I don't think we can share straws. They have our cooties." And we went back to playing.

Mike was not having this. He grabbed a new straw and swallowed his medicine so he could play. Everyone won that game.

As a child, I accompanied my magician father, Irv Weiner, when he clowned at a local children's hospital. The sound of laughter from kids in wheelchairs and hospital beds left me with a lasting memory that has shaped my professional life.

I studied early childhood education along with special needs and started out as a pre-school teacher and workshop facilitator. I loved being in the moment with the children I taught. Later, I moved on to run a daycare program from my home. All along I did not realize that my ability to observe and understand children, along with my silliness and play, is just what hospital clowns do.

Years later the bulb lit up. An opportunity to train with Jeannie Lindheim was available, and I started hospital clowning at MGH and Franciscan Hospital for Children. I have been Tic Toc with Hearts & Noses Hospital Clown Troupe since 1999. I took on the job of executive director in 2005.

Website: *http://www.heartsandnoses.org/*

Chapter 17
Joe 'Tiny' Luce

There Is Such a Thing as a Free Lunch

On the way home from our hospital visitation, still in clown character, I entered the fast-food drive-thru. Accustomed to curious eyes while in clown, I noticed the man's intense stare from his rearview mirror ahead of me. Unable to discern whether he was friend or foe, I was getting slightly uneasy while waiting behind him. He picked up his food. He saluted, and I waved as he drove away. I approached the cashier's window and learned the gentleman ahead of me paid for my meal.

Two things came to mind.

1. I would never presume to think a clown deserves the same level of respect as professionals willing to risk their lives in the service of others (firemen,

policemen, veterans) but that day I got a tiny taste of the appreciation like they experience, and it tasted good.

2. I wish I had known someone else was paying. I would have ordered the apple pie too.

In the Waiting Room

Picture a crowded hospital waiting room as a mother enters with a toddler and a teen-ager. Before too long, the mother went for tests, and the toddler wanted to go with her but was left in the care of his disengaged sister. Toddler protested loudly, and his volume increased exponentially as the sister ignored him. Her hoodie pulled over her head with the drawstring pulled down in front leaving just the size of a cell phone opening.

Meanwhile, the toddler's screeching almost reached dog-hearing levels. Other people waiting exchanged alarmed looks. You could almost read the thought clouds above their heads: Send a search party for the mother! Shake the teen-ager back to the present! Where did I put those earplugs?!

But wait, have no fear, the super clown is here! Without regard for his own safety, super clown rushed into action armed with only his wits and bare hands performing an extended version of the invisible jumping flea routine.

Even the teen-ager had come out of her soundproof hoodie and laughed along with the toddler. As the nurse called me in for my appointment, many silent thank-you's were mouthed. I felt more like a real clown at that moment than if I had performed for hundreds of my own colleagues.

Peace restored.

Joe Luce: "I once wrote a book on elephants. Paper would have been better."

Facebook: *https://www.facebook.com/joe.luce.79*

Chapter 18
Greg 'Mister Greggy' McMahan

My Most Embarrassing Show

High school. By this time, I had been doing magic a little over a year and had done a couple of paid shows. I even had business cards (hand drawn on blank-back playing cards). I was a professional! It was time for me to hit the big time.

I arranged a meeting with the principal and somehow persuaded him to book me for a school assembly program for my entire high school. How much was I to be paid? It depended on how many tickets were sold at 25 cents each.

I was very excited about this and worked on a show right away. It soon became clear I had about fifteen minutes' worth of material. The show was to be forty-five minutes. In two weeks, I had a lot of work to do.

I called a friend from the local teen magic club, "The Counts of Conjuring" (of which I was the president). His name was Don, and he was 19. I was 16 or 17. Don had been doing magic for two years now, and he had 20 minutes of material, which included a zombie routine (all the rage back then, along with dancing canes). Together we had a thirty-five-minute show. We're getting closer. Upon calling him, I learned that he had just built a sub-trunk. I was ecstatic. We had an illusion for the show! He agreed to do a show with me, we'd split the money. Then the next step—the big time.

As I practiced my fifteen-minute show, he practiced his twenty. Neither of us had enough space to practice the sub-trunk, so I used the stage at the school one evening while a sports awards banquet was going on in another room. We got to the school, unloaded our equipment, and set up. When ready, we each practiced our act, helping one another to fine tune and improve our show.

With that out of the way, we brought out the sub-trunk. Don demonstrated the canvas sack with the gimmicked metal rod going thru the holes in the top, and the hinged flap in the back of the sub-trunk. As I later learned, Don did not know how the actual illusion worked, so he made up his own version.

Just as we were about to practice the illusion routine, the principal sticks his head in the room and said we had to leave, because the banquet was over. We were a bit concerned because we had not practiced the trick. He said too bad, but we had to leave. We left all our stuff there, ready to return the next day for our show, which was to take place first thing in the morning.

Next day, we got there early, but couldn't get into the gym yet. Once in, we barely had time to get into costume and load the doves (one each). The crowd came in and quickly filled the gym. It was loud, and we realized that we had never even considered microphones. Don had a portable tape player with which to play the music, just barely powerful enough for a small living room.

I opened the show. To say I was nervous is an understatement. I was petrified, terrified, literally shaking. It suddenly dawned on me that every person in the audience knew me, and I would be with them every day for the next three years.

I began my routine. I remember little about the show, except that some tricks worked. There was no reaction from the audience, and I was going really fast. Really, really fast. My fifteen-minute routine ended after six minutes.

Next up was Don. I have no idea what he did. I was backstage, in shock. Once he finished (also going too fast—his twenty minutes turned into twelve) I dragged the trunk on stage. No wheels.

So here we were, eighteen minutes into a forty-five-minute show . . . twenty-seven minutes to perform an illusion we've never practiced. With the trapdoor in the wrong place. In front of a room full of teen-agers. With three years of experience between us.

I began by asking for a volunteer from the audience to come up and examine the trunk. Nobody seemed interested. Go figure. I looked straight at my best friend Richard and again asked for somebody to come up and help. He shook his head no. I walked out into the audience, asked Richard to come up and help while grabbing his arm and dragging him up to the stage. This resulted in the first reaction from the audience, a smattering of laughter.

Once Richard was on stage, glaring at me, I asked him to hit the sides of the trunk. When he got to the trapdoor, he asked what that was. I directed him to the other side of the trunk. Once he was done, Richard literally ran back to his seat. I wished I could have joined him.

Time to begin the trick. I put the gimmicked handcuff on Don and then had him step into the canvas sack. So far, so good. This part we had practiced. I slid the metal rod thru the holes in the bag and secured a padlock on each end. This wasn't so bad.

Now to get Don into the trunk which was about four feet high. It's difficult lifting a person encased in a bag up and over into a trunk. I finally hoisted him up onto my shoulder and flopped him down into the trunk. When he landed, with a loud thud, I heard him yell ouch. I was briefly concerned that I had just killed him until I heard him moan in pain.

I closed the lid and put the locks into the clasps. We were now about four or five minutes into the routine, and it hasn't been too bad. Yet.

I jumped onto the top, ready to do the magical change, standing there not knowing what to do next. Then I remembered. Isn't there supposed to be a sheet or something to cover the transposition? I jumped off the trunk, ran backstage to grab anything I could find. In the prop room was a tablecloth. It would have to do. I ran back onstage, climbed back on the trunk, and opened the cloth in front of me. It was quite a coincidence that the tablecloth was the same width as the trunk.

I lifted the cloth in front of my face, then lowered it down counting. "One." Again, "Two." A quick glance down. No Don. Slower this time, "Three." Still no Don. "Four . . . Five." By now I'm staring at my feet, waiting. Finally, I signal to Don ("OK, I'm ready. Roll on out now.") and he rolls out the back of the box, onto the floor. Because of the matching sizes of the cloth and the trunk, everybody in the center of the audience is unaware that Don is on the floor behind the trunk, while everybody else on the sides can see him plain as day. And they make sure we know they can see him. Don finally crawls up onto the trunk, in full view of the crowd. I had lost interest by this point and dropped the cloth on the floor.

We jumped down off the trunk, take a bow to dead silence, and walk offstage. We're done. And only twenty minutes left in the show.

I didn't go to school for a week after that. It was the most horrible, embarrassing experience of my life. It was the closest I ever came to giving up magic entirely. But in the end, I stuck with it. I figured after that, anything else that went wrong would be nothing in comparison. It couldn't get any worse. And it never did.

Balloon Show

I once showed up at a small gig with a bag of balloons, a balloon pump, and a folding table ready to teach about fifteen kids how to make balloon animals. When I was shown into the room, there were about seventy-five people sitting in bleachers expecting a full forty-five-minute show.

Usually this would not have been a problem except my showcase was at home. Uh oh. As I'm setting up the

table and greeting the crowd, I decided to teach everyone how to make a balloon animal. That's why I was
hired, right? However, I had to make blowing up seventy-five balloons entertaining. Within forty-five minutes. Then teach them all to twist.

I started out doing all the warmups I could think of.
Some of them involved getting tangled up in my vest.
Then my suspenders. Some crowd interaction fun.
Next, I searched my brain's database for any comedy
bits I could do with a volunteer from the audience.
Remember, during all this time I'm also blowing up
balloon after balloon and wrapping them with another
balloon in bundles of about 10 each.

Some bits I remember doing were these:

1. Being scared of the noise my electric balloon
   pump made.

2. Getting the volunteer to hold as many balloons
   as possible.

3. "Accidentally" letting go of a balloon.

4. Shooting the balloon from my finger and making
   it stick to the ceiling.

5. And many more that I've since forgotten.

Once everybody had a balloon, it was smooth sailing as I had a set routine for teaching the twisting. However, it was the first time with seventy-five people, so I slowed it down and enlisted the service of some adults to help the younger kids in the crowd.

I ended up doing over an hour, and the people in charge were thrilled. The audience laughed a lot, had a blast making the balloons, and I had a new show. It was a big boost for me.

It would have been a lot easier if I had my showcase in the car, but then I wouldn't have gained the self-confidence to know I can handle unexpected situations and make them work.

However, I always have my showcase in the car after that.'

I have since chronicled this show, after a lot of refinements and updates, in my book "Balloon Shows" available on my website.

Born at an early age, Greg McMahan loved performing as long as he can remember. As a teen, Greg developed an interest in magic and other circus skills.

He's written instructional books for children's entertainers worldwide and conducted seminars and lectures.

Since 1992, Greg has taught magic to thousands of children at Circus Camp.

In 2003 Greg traveled with the Cole Bros Circus as their national spokesperson. Greg promoted the circus on TV and radio stations and newspaper interviews plus live appearances.

Now performing in Atlanta as "Mister Greggy," Greg loves seeing the smiles on his audience's faces!

Website : *http://www.mistergreggy.com/*

Chapter 19
Taylor 'Hoops' Moss

Grateful to Make People Happy

There is no way I could list just one gratifying experience from my clowning adventures. Every single time I get to interact with a person as Hoops, I have the opportunity to affect how they feel about clowns by being myself. I take that responsibility seriously. Making people, kids and adults, laugh and smile while treating them with respect is my goal. It makes my heart happy to see others happy. Hoops makes people feel happy. That makes me grateful.

Let the Kids Approach the Clown

The most challenging thing I face as a clown is older kids or adults preventing younger kids from getting to me. Kids are naturally drawn to clowns. It's natural for a child to want to see something different and something they don't see every day. They are curious because they are kids. They are full of genuine wonder. They are drawn to me specifically, I think, because I am approachable in makeup and costume and, let's face it, because I am a kid myself.

When I see a young child, the first thing I want to do is make them smile or laugh. Sometimes that connection is blocked because the older person exposes their fear, real or exaggerated, for the younger child to hear or sense. To battle this problem, I look to other kids. I turn my attention to those other children and make them a balloon, let them try my Hula Hoops, or play a game. Seeing other children playing and having fun usually gets the hesitant child to forget their concerns.

It's okay to be a little scared about things as a kid or as an adult. It's not okay to let your fear prevent another person from having a good experience. I don't have the power as Hoops or as Taylor to stop that from happening (as much as I want to), so I just have to continue to make people smile. Make them laugh. And treat them with respect.

Classical training in both dance and voice is merely the start of what makes Taylor Moss one to watch as her career is taking shape! At fourteen years old, she is a versatile actress, vocalist, dancer, model, and variety performer.

Taylor recently starred in the award-winning films, The Ark, Knock Knock, *and* Tsirk, *all directed by Mark Rosenau. She also completed filming on several other films, including starring in* Cries Unheard. *In addition to acting and dance classes, year-round training with professional circus performers and vocal training elevate her skills to the next level. She is an exceptional athlete.*

Taylor's dream is to one day run away and join the circus, but she loves performing more than anything. She loves to study Russian culture and has attended several Russian immersion language camps.

Website: *http://tayloramoss.com*
Email: *taylor@tayloramoss.com*

Chapter 20
Sharon 'Toots' Nelson

Finding the Lost Smile

It was in August of about 1993 when I was a very new clown. I belonged to my first clown club, Comedy Caravan Clown Club, which met in New Hope, Minnesota.

Since I had taken classes for makeup and skits, the club invited me to join them. As a member of the Comedy Caravan Club, I had the opportunity to receive more clown education.

As August was approaching, clowns informed me that August is known as Clown Month. We would do extra events that month by touring the city of New Hope and businesses in that area. We were going to a large and well-known nursing home in that area. I was a little apprehensive because my experience in nursing homes was rather limited.

We arrived at the nursing home, where the staff said we could visit the residents. Okay, I thought, here I go. I talked to a few residents and found myself in front of this elderly gentleman sitting in a wheelchair. He didn't look thrilled to have us at his home. I wondered why.

I took a deep breath and said, "Good afternoon. I belong to the clown club and we have come here to visit with you for a little while."

No response. He looked at me without changing his expression. I tried once again with the same response.

Then I tried again by asking him, "Where is your smile?"

Again, the same response.

By this time, he had become my challenge for the day. "Where is your smile?" I said again.

No response.

Now I really felt the need to make him smile, so I said while putting my hand into my pocket, "Oh goodness, I found your smile it was right here in my pocket."

Wow, I finally got a smile out of him.

After we visited with a few other residents for a brief time, a staff member asked, "How did you get him to smile? It has been a very long time since anyone has gotten that response from him."

I realized I had found my calling to continue being a clown to make others happy while having so much fun myself.

Clown Down

It was May 10, 2014. A senior citizen group had invited members of one of my clown clubs to a church about three hours from my home. We started out about 8:30 a.m. I was riding with Cora and another female clown (who had grown up in the area we were going), and two male clowns each drove on their own, one with his wife and the other transporting some larger equipment we would use. We would do an after-lunch entertainment for this senior citizen group.

We arrived in time to set up for our show before the luncheon was to be served to the seniors. Because we did not want to be eating with the group while in costume, three of us took in a viewing of the large waterfall in the area. Cora's sister-in-law guided us to the falls.

Arriving, we saw a family having a picnic lunch, so we stopped to say hi.

As we walked over to the falls, someone suggested the clowns go nearer the falls to have our picture taken. I did not feel comfortable doing this, because I am afraid of heights. I said, "No."

While Cora and I were standing just looking at the falls, we realized that the male clown had taken the path to the area right above the falls. Wow, I thought, he is getting pretty close. Then I realized that he wanted to get a good picture of the falls.

I watched as he got closer and was standing on the rocks. I also watched as he took one step closer, not realizing that the rock he would step on was a little lower than he thought. Yes, down he fell! He looked like a rag doll with his arms and legs outstretched floating thru the air, hitting small trees just missing some larger rocks. During this time, all I could do was scream. "No! No! No!"

He fell onto the ground below with the lower part of his body in the water and his head on the sand. I thought he might be dead but after about a minute he moved. Thank goodness he was alive. But now how badly was he hurt? How was he going to get out as there were cliffs surrounding the whole area?

Cora's sister-in-law borrowed a cell phone from a young couple and called 9-1-1. She reported that a clown (he was in costume) had fallen over the falls and we needed help.

The rescue team arrived and made their plans on how to rescue him. They lowered one of their team along with a basket-type gurney and got him out. Before the rescue was complete, Cora, and I decided I was to return to the church and inform our other member that he and I would put on the show while Cora stayed at the park to be with our friend while they rescued him.

We quickly changed the show from a four-person show to a two-person show. Thank goodness both of us were experienced clowns. In about fifteen minutes we got our act together and put on a forty-five-minute show. The seniors loved us.

Our friend was airlifted to a major hospital and survived the fall.

As Cora and I were making the three-hour trip home, we stopped for some ice cream. While we were eating our ice cream and Cora was driving, her cell phone rang. She pulled over to the side of the road to answer the call. While we were stopped, a gentleman pulled up behind us to see if we were okay. We responded yes and thanked him.

A couple minutes later, while Cora was still on the phone, a police officer also stopped and was walking toward us on my side of the car. I rolled down the window and said, "Hi."

The officer took one look at me still in costume, eating a cone, and said, "Oh, are you OK?" I told him my friend had a phone call and pulled over to answer it. My answer pleased him. He then wanted to know where we had been and where we were going.

After such a trying day we both had to laugh and still do to this day.

I have now clowned for close to twenty-six years and now belong to two clown clubs: "The Clown Arounds" and "The ClownCare Club." Most of my clowning in the last few years has been in nursing homes, community events, and some church events. In the past, I did parades along with the nursing homes, battered women's shelters, and clown ministry as a solo clown.

I enjoy working with my friends in both clubs and thoroughly enjoy performing for children of all ages.

Email: *toots4344@yahoo.com*

Chapter 21
Kristi 'Krickey' Parker

A Fire Alarm Birthday

Today, I had an interesting experience at a birthday party. Out of about one hundred fifty guests, thirty-five or so were kids. The party was held at a big event hall connected to a restaurant. It was fully catered, with magnificent decorations and an amazing cake. They hired me, a face painter, a deejay, a photographer, and a videographer—you get the idea.

Midway through the party, the building's fire alarm went off. Everybody put on their coats and went outside in the thirty-degree weather to wait for the fire department to arrive. Turns out that the popcorn machine they had set up was right underneath a smoke detector, and the steam caused the alarm to go off. Eventually the party resumed, and all was well.

As the alarm was going off, I was thinking to myself, "If the building is on fire, what clown stuff should I grab?" I had brought all kinds of stuff with me, but I decided the bag that contained the magic tricks and my balloon bag would be the things I would rescue. Most of the other stuff was props I made and could replace if necessary. Thankfully, I have a hidden pocket built into my costume where I keep my license, car key, and phone.

After today's adventure, I will make sure I always keep my keys and so forth in that pocket should I need to make a hasty exit!

It was a party for one-year-old twins! I had been asked to do my show, which includes music, silly magic, and a puppet. Normally my show is twenty minutes, and I round out the hour doing balloons.

They wanted two hours, which included the show, games with prizes, and balloons. (They originally wanted me to do the face painting as well, so I had to explain that although I'm a multi-talented clown, I don't have super powers!)

When I arrived, people were eating, so I went from table to table, interacting with the kids. When I asked the mom when I should start the show, she said to do balloons first. Sigh. I knew what would happen! I got stuck doing balloons the whole time.

The show probably wouldn't have gone over well anyway because there wasn't a big space, and music was blaring. There was lots of commotion, and adults were talking loudly. Sigh. It was fun, but not at all what I expected—and the fire alarm just made it all the more interesting!

In the end the lady seemed happy and gave me a good tip. (I did end up staying an extra forty minutes, due to the fire alarm.) I guess I was the most disappointed because I really have fun interacting with the kids at the show and missed out on that. Balloons are fine, but don't showcase my talent.

I guess I should have asked more questions of the mother about the venue and the setup when I was confirming the booking over the phone. In a situation like that, it would have worked out better to have a separate room for the kids so I could do my show.

I did bring my little mike and PA system, thinking there might be adult chatter in the background, but the second I walked in, I knew that wasn't going to work. After asking lots of questions about the ages of the child guests and how many kids to expect, I agreed to do the show because there were lots of kids of all ages. In the past, I did a one-year-old birthday party, and none of the kids was older than two and a half. That was a disaster. Never again!

I'm always telling people how much I love being a clown. The joy I can give to people comes back at me tenfold. It fills my heart and soul!

Winning over a Clown-Skeptic

This is one of my favorite experiences.

A mom hired me to entertain at her daughter's fifth birthday party. It was in the summer, so the circus-themed party was outside in the yard. There was a bouncy house, cotton candy, popcorn, a huge cake, and even pony rides!

As soon as I arrived, the birthday child's grandmother came running up to me with a sense of urgency. She pointed out one of the young guests, the birthday girl's cousin, and informed me that the child was deathly afraid of clowns. I assured the elderly woman I never approach anyone who seems to be afraid of me, and it was OK for her granddaughter to watch from a distance.

I started out with my clown show, engaging the children with songs, silly magic, and some puppet antics. I noticed the little girl whom I had been warned about, sitting way in the back in the last row, snuggled up next to her grandmother, but she was singing and smiling right along with everyone else.

After the show, the children all lined up to have balloon animals made. The little shy girl got in line with the others, and when she came up to me, I did not treat her any differently than any of the other guests. My clown's personality is gentle, caring, and loving. I try not to be too loud or boisterous, so that most people feel comfortable approaching me. I asked the little girl what animal she wanted, and she got to pick her favorite color. She skipped away happily, hugging her balloon creation.

When it was time to leave the party, I called out my farewell to a chorus of goodbye's and thank you's from the crowd. Suddenly the little child who was supposedly deathly afraid ran up to me, wrapped her arms around my legs, looked up with her big blue eyes and shouted "I love you, clown!"

Grandma was flabbergasted, the little girl was beaming, and my heart grew three sizes that day!

Kristi "Krickey" Parker has been delighting audiences from Maine to Mexico with her crazy antics, silly songs, playful puppets, and kooky magic since 2007. Kristi is grateful to have had the opportunity to learn her craft from some of the most highly respected and talented clowns in the country.

She has trained numerous times at Mooseburger Clown Arts Camp, Bubba University, and the American Clown Academy, as well as many local clown related workshops and seminars.

Krickey is an active member of the Granite State Clown Alley, in addition to holding the position of World Clown Association Northeast Regional Director. She continues to share ideas, encourage First of Mays, and spread the joy of clowning wherever she goes.

Website: *http://www.krickeytheclown.com/*

Chapter 22
Dena 'DeeNee,' 'Flossie' Piraino

A Tale of Two Cities: Hungry for Scent

 My Adventures in Clowning stories go hand in hand, because they occurred on the same weekend in two very different settings.

It was in the early 1990s in December. On a Saturday, I was hired to do walk-around clowning on Rodeo Drive in Beverly Hills. Upon my arrival and check-in, I found out I would go out to a particular area of shops and hand out perfume samples. Hey, why not? I was getting paid.

So off I went with my little basket of free perfume samples. You would think I was giving away a million dollars (which in Beverly Hills is chump change!). Grabbing hands mauled me!

After five minutes, I went back to "base camp" and asked for more samples. They looked at me as if I had put all the first batch in my own pocket! They gave me more, and off I went.

More hand grabbing! I could not believe what I was experiencing! These rich people were greedy and took more than one free perfume sample. After about a half-hour of refilling, the samples were all gone.

I still had time left to clown, so then I just did my thing, thankful I didn't have hands pawing at me anymore.

A Tale of Two Cities: Generous with Gifts

The next day, I volunteered my time at a Salvation Army Christmas party in Anaheim, California along with several other clowns.

The day began with carnival-type games for the kids, which we clowns helped with and participated in. Disneyland donated the prizes. They weren't anything to write home about—mostly small, outdated promo giveaways from the park. But those kids could not be happier with their winnings. (Their big prize came later from Santa!)

At one point, I fake-cried with some kids because I wasn't winning anything. The kids felt sorry for me and shared their little trinkets with me. This warmed my heart.

I immediately thought back to the day before when those rich people of Beverly Hills were pawing at me to get a free perfume sample. And now these kids from modest backgrounds were sharing their little trinkets with DeeNee.

What a tale of two cities.

Dena "DeeNee," "Flossie" Piraino holds a B.A. in Theatre Arts. She, along with her mom and dad, opened "Under the Big Top," a clown supply business in 1986. She has traveled the country clowning, selling and teaching the art of clowning. She has only recently semi-retired from performing and selling. She still loves teaching and sharing her love of clowning.

Email: *underthebigtop1@hotmail.com*

Chapter 23
Nicole 'Maggie' Portwood

Gratifying to See Someone Smile

My most gratifying experience in clowning comes from one thing— seeing someone smile. Sound like a cliché? Maybe, but it is sincerely why we clowns do what we do.

Many clowns will say you catch the bug when you first put on that red nose and see someone giggle.

Historically, we have been the entertainer of the young, but I find I make a connection with *everyone* I encounter and spend a moment with. It is in just a moment that a special bond can be formed.

It is a curious thing even to me, who experience it daily, but clowns emit a joy that is unexplainable. Clowns say, "It's time to have fun!" It's time to forget anything that might be sad in your life, even if it's just for a few moments.

We seem to make friends wherever we go. We give people the hope that there is still good in the world. I have had spontaneous hugs from people I didn't even know, simply because I was a clown. I am loved!

Maybe that's why we do it? I feel just as special as those who I am trying to make feel special.

Yes, I think that is the most gratifying thing about being a clown—I make them smile and they make *me* smile!

Frustrating Fear of Clowns

Clearly for me the most frustrating thing about being a clown is the present day "fear of clowns."

This is something of a more modern phenomenon as I did not experience this at all in my beginning years as a clown. I grew up with Bozo, Ronald McDonald, The Town Clown on Captain Kangaroo, and of course the countless clowns I would see when I attended the circus.

Never did I think that children would be exposed to frightening movies that would influence them to dislike something that is only meant for good. So with that in mind, when I encounter a child that has been misled, I offer understanding.

That comes in many forms depending on the severity of the apparent aversion. If the child is approachable, I simply offer whatever it is I am doing at the time, whether it be a balloon, magic, or a juggling trick.

If it is an older child or teen, I will often ask them why they are afraid, and of course, the most popular response is that they watched a movie they shouldn't have. I explain that I am sorry they had to experience that, but as they can see, I do not look anything like what is in those films.

I ask them if they would like to learn more about the art of clowning or if they would like to learn a magic trick. Basically, anything that closes the door on that conversation, so we can move on to the fun! I am successful most of the time.

The rare occasion I am not successful happens because some children don't come close enough for me to chat with them. It is then that my job is the most frustrating. I must resign myself to the fact that there is someone I couldn't make smile that day, and that makes me very sad.

Nicole Portwood, AKA "Maggie the Clown," a thirty-four-year veteran of clowning, attended Ringling Bros. Clown College and spent four years traveling nationally and internationally with

The Greatest Show on Earth. Career highlights include working for Disneyland, Disney World, and The International Clown Festival in India and teaching at renowned clown conventions and camps.

She currently clowns at parties, schools, libraries, and corporate events and teaches through her Bay State Clown Arts, offering private clown tutoring in a personal training setting.

Website: *https://www.maggietheclown.com/*

Chapter 24
Judy 'Dear Heart' Quest

Making a Last Birthday Remarkable

 My most gratifying stories center on hospital clowning. For years I was on call when a child would have his or her last birthday in the hospital. My props had to be sterilized. I gowned up over my costume and entertained the whole family.

My son is popular. He is a spectacular juggler, so he often came along. On one occasion, my son and I celebrated the birthday of an eight-year-old. The child did not appear to be ill. We did our act. He and his mother enjoyed the show.

A few days later we received a hand-decorated thank you which read, "Dear Heart, you were pretty good, but your son was *awesome!*" The child died a week later. We were blessed to be there and celebrate his life.

The Frightened Child Upstairs

A challenging situation took place at a birthday party when the child stayed upstairs and cried the entire time of the party.

When I have dealt with frightened children, I have been able to bring them around by using older children to show that there is nothing to fear. I have experienced many shy children, but I am usually successful in having them come around by the end of the show.

On this occasion, I never even saw the child, yet he howled during the whole show. This made the other children so uncomfortable that I had a hard time getting volunteers or engaging them in the show. A big part of the problem was that it was primarily an adult party with lots of noise and drinking.

I tried everything I could think of, but the whole thing was a disaster.

What I took away from this was that when booking parties, I lay out clear guidelines for adults. They can either take part in the show or be in another room where they don't disturb the party.

Judy Quest has worked with people with disabilities and lectured all over the country on the topic. She has been clowning in Omaha, Nebraska, since 1982 and has served on the board of

Clowns of American International (COAI) for two different periods, serving as President from 1998 to 2000. She was also COAI Clown of the Year in 2008 and loves to compete in paradability and teach clowning.

Email: *dearheart@cox.net*

Chapter 25
Anand N. 'Huggy Bear' Sharma

A Million and One Days

As I was hospital clowning, I met an elderly woman who held my hand, with tears in her eyes, saying in a trembling voice, "Honey, you know my days are numbered."

I placed my other hand on her delicate, wrinkled hands carefully kissed it and replied, "Yes darling, your days are indeed numbered. You have one million and one days more to live."

She hesitated for a second, then her face miraculously transformed from someone terrified of her impending death a few seconds ago to a hearty and guffawing long laugh. Over the next few minutes, we shared jokes and laughed a lot. She said, "Bless you for saying such a positive thing and making me laugh for the first time in months." I left, wiping tears from my eyes, with her precious words of blessing.

Four Hours of Tears

Today was one of the toughest four hours of my hospital clowning career.

1. One woman just walked up, hugged me, and cried. I cried along with her. She thanked me and left.

2. I spent about twenty minutes with a young couple. The husband is a soldier in the U.S. Army and he told me his story while I held his weeping wife's hand all the while.

3. A lady in severe pain laughed with me, with tears rolling down both our eyes.

Today, I saw more people with sadness and tears than ever before. Crying along with the patients and their loved ones, I am so blessed I could lend my shoulder to them when they needed it most.

I Never Saw This Coming

There was a sweet patient who just loved me and the idea of hospital clowning so much that she wanted to join me and visit the other patients in the hospital. She refused to listen when I politely told her she cannot accompany me.

Before I knew it, she removed the tube from her arms and went to the restroom to dress up. I rushed out of her room and told a nurse. She sternly told her the hospital does not allow her to go to other patient's rooms. The patient was not at all happy that I called for the nurse. The nurses were not thrilled about the situation either. I think they blamed me for the upset. I know I did the right thing by getting staff immediately. It was one awkward incident, causing stress to the patient and the nursing staff.

I am still struggling to figure out what could I have done differently on that day.

I am an engineer by accident and a certified clown by choice. I am a volunteer caring clown. As a digital design engineer, I have worked in technology and computers for over twenty-five years. I have done more than fifty theater appearances as a child actor. I emigrated from India and have become part of the melting pot of America.

Facebook: *https://facebook.com/HuggyBearClown/*

Chapter 26
Irene 'SlugbugZ' Spudic

In Memory of Shygumshoe

 In October 2010, I was attending clown class! I was excited that I was going to become a clown, but not many people knew. I work at a hospital, and for many years prior to becoming a clown, I always wore crazy sox and bright-colored shoes, so I was well-known by everyone.

One day, a lady I knew well asked why I loved wearing my crazy sox and shoes. I told her it must be the clown in me. I explained that I was going to clown school and was getting ready to graduate soon. Her face lit up, and she said, "Are you serious? Because I'm a clown too!"

She went to the same school with Janet "Jellybean" Tucker, who was also my teacher/mentor. She was a member of the Calumet Clowns.

I was so excited to find out that someone I knew was also a clown. She asked me what day I would graduate, and I told her October 25. To my surprise, she showed up to my graduation and gave me my first bag of magic tricks as a **gift**. From that time on, we became good friends, and at my first Midwest Clown Convention in LaPorte, Indiana, in 2011, she was there and inspired me to get into the makeup competition.

This was my **first time** being in front of an audience of people and judges, to **be judged** on my makeup and costume. I was one nervous clown! She told me to keep my eyes on her so I wouldn't be nervous, and I did. To my surprise, on award night, they announced my name for **first** place. I was so surprised and happy because I was a first-time, first-try, first-place winner!

Since then, I've attended the Midwest Clown Convention, and I've competed in several competitions and won several first-, second-, and third-place awards every year.

Shygumshoe was my inspiration, and we continued attending conventions until she was **diagnosed** with lung cancer. I, too, become a member of the Calumet Clowns, where we volunteered to do a benefit for her. She was so **thankful** and touched by all we did. I had a great time and feeling of joy to **be able to** help someone I truly cared about and loved.

I had done several benefits for people I did not know personally, and it made me feel happy that I was able to help, but knowing this special person personally was an experience I'll never forget! Sadly, Shygumshoe passed away in 2014.

Doing benefits is close to our hearts for this reason. At another cancer walk, our whole group wore shirts with her face. Team Shygumshoe!!

Say What?

It was a beautiful 4th of July day. I was so excited to be in a parade with my Calumet Clown Alley. I brought along my weenie dog Oscar as my walk-around, or should I say, he was pretty much walking me! This parade was over an hour long. We were about halfway to the end, and I was having a great time with all the children, introducing them to Oscar, telling them how I call him Frank, and he's a pure-bred, 100-percent beef, and so on, when all of a sudden, this big burley man storms out of the crowd, and came directly towards me, right in my face, and yelled a horrible obscenity at me.

My whole body felt stunned for a moment, and I knew I had to quickly keep moving. I didn't know if he was coming after me, but I didn't look back to find out. I knew I needed to immediately gather myself since no one else ahead of me saw what happened, and even though I wanted to run to the end, the more I continued with my bit, the more relieved I became.

That was a day I'll never forget.

Irene Burgos Spudic graduated from clown school on October 25, 2010, and her clown character SlugbugZ was born! She is member of the Calumet, Michiana, and Krazy Clown Klub. Irene participated in several events at her home church, performed for the Ronald McDonald house, Children's Miracle Network, and nursing homes, as well as doing hospital visits, and parades. She designs her costumes and has won several competitions in makeup, skits, and paradability, at the MCA, and WCA conventions. Irene Burgo Spudic was inducted into the MCA Hall of Fame in 2017. The Red nose now runs in my family. Bump a Nose!

Chapter 27
Jane 'Cotton Candy' Welch-Sprague

Trick-E

A favorite clown time for me is clowning at "Kids' Expos" where I do walk-arounds, holding a fancy box, which they can't see inside, filled with "Brown Es." I ask the child if they would like a brownie I made that morning? Of course, they say yes, though some ask a parent first. Then I hand them a BROWN E (the letter E cut out of brown paper) the look on their face is priceless as the parents start laughing. The child thinks about it for a moment and usually catches on and starts laughing. They are then excited to play the trick on someone they know.

It's a fun and easy thing for a clown to do, and it works for young and old. The adults enjoy it just as much. I tell them it has no calories and is high in fiber. I love the feeling I get from making people laugh and smile.

But I'm Not a Scary Clown

The worst incident, and I have not had many, is when a person is afraid of me dressed as a clown and runs from me. It makes me sad when that happens. Usually it is a grown person. If they will let me talk with them, I will try to help them realize I am a good clown and want to make people smile.

My takeaway is for some people it is a real fear and it is hard to change that fear for them. It upsets me that there are so many bad images of clowns and time hurts the good, happy ones.

Jane "Cotton Candy" Welch-Sprague has been clowning for six years in Boise, Idaho. Her clown name is Cotton Candy because she loves it. Since I was a child, I always wanted to be a clown. I also volunteer at Zoo Boise, where I get to interact with the animals and guests. I am married and retired from working at a nonprofit. I love traveling the world and visiting my grandchildren and great-grandchildren.

Email: *TahitiJane@msn.com*

Chapter 28
Ted 'Twaddles' White

Dealing with Loss

I began my clowning activity as a hospital clown. I loved the challenge of approaching a room with no idea of what I was about to confront, having only a few minutes to read the specific audience, and then coming up with something that will entertain them.

In this environment, the only certainty is that you can expect the unexpected. One has to be ready to respond immediately and react to the person or persons in the room. Sometimes the parents, particularly the upset mother of a small, sick child, needs to be distracted more than the child.

The most bizarre experience for me started one day at a local private hospital. I entered a room where a man, aged about his late sixties, was the patient. Sitting be-side the bed was his distraught wife.

I quickly understood that the patient, we'll call him Barry, did not want to be entertained, but just wanted to talk. After asking about my costume, makeup and how I became a clown, he told me about himself.

He had been a professional opera singer. He had per-formed in all the famous opera houses around the world and was on first-name terms with Pavarotti, Domingo, Carrera, and more.

Then Barry, pleased to have the opportunity, told me about what his wife clearly didn't want him to talk about to her.

Barry was a diabetic. This affected his health, and the doctors had just amputated one of his legs. He was accepting and upbeat about the whole thing. He was looking forward to getting out of the hospital. as for the future he thought he "might have to just *hop* into it." We happily chatted on for longer than a normal clown-patient visit.

About eight months later, I was with a group of clowns at a street party when someone yelled "Twaddles!"

I looked around, and there was Barry. He was in good spirit and was handling the prosthetic leg well. He was now the volunteer musical director of the Buderim Male Choir.

We had a humorous conversation about the fact that with the peg leg, when it rained, he was just an old stick in the mud, and so forth. Both agreed that it was wonderful to have met up again.

Six months later, at the same private hospital, I entered a room and there were Barry and his again traumatized wife.

He greeted me like an old friend, and he immediately shocked his wife by saying, "I always knew these private hospitals can cost an arm and a leg, but these blighters have taken both my legs."

We had a fine time—sharing sick jokes like "No need to drink alcohol at the party, legless when you arrive." After a while, even his wife was laughing. Anyone overhearing, who did not understand the back-story, would be mortified, but it is what Barry and his wife needed on that specific occasion.

I was born 1940 in Rockhampton, Queensland, Australia. After leaving high school, I had the experience of something like seventeen changes in careers. At age sixty -five I finally found what I wanted to do with my life–be a clown. I joined a local alley, joined Clowns of American International (COAI) in 2008. Attended the Red Skelton Clown School in 2010 and returned to Vincennes in

2013 for the Red Skelton 100th anniversary celebration. I've been the COAI International Regional Vice President since 2014.

In 2017 I, along with my bestest friend Heather "Pockets" Wuersching, commenced clowning together as Twaddles & Pockets. We clown mostly in aged-care facilities.

Chapter 29
Mark F. 'Mr. Who Ha'
Willimann, Esq.

Too Sick to Laugh

 I performed my "How A Clown Becomes a Clown," show at the M.D. Anderson Children's Cancer Hospital in Houston, Texas. I was not prepared for what I saw as my audience—about 40-plus children wheeling around bottles of IV with tubes in their arms. Many were bald because of the chemotherapy, some were wheeled in their beds and had to turn their heads to see me. It was heart-wrenching to see these kids suffering. So I did my show, and the normal laugh points I had become accustomed to did not materialize with this audience. It was an eerie silence, except from some staff members or family that were visiting.

At the end of my show, I dejectedly put all my props and equipment into my trunk, and one kid came up to give me a hug—IV bottle, tubes, and all. She told me my show was great, which sort of startled me because of the lack of feedback from the group.

As I was leaving, a nurse stopped me to tell me that the kids and the adults said it was a great show. When I asked why there was so little reaction to my performance, she responded: Most are too sick to laugh, but I knew they were enjoying it because they were *smiling*! (You'd never think folks could be too sick to laugh.)

The Case of the Purloined Trunk

I once performed my show for a Blue and Gold Cub Scout Dinner. Before my show, I'm dressed like a regular guy, with T-shirt and shorts. My trunk is by my side. And I'm waiting for my introduction. I turn to speak to the organizer about when I will take the stage, and when I looked down, I saw that someone had taken my trunk. All my juggling equipment, make-up, costume, everything except my unicycle. Just then, the MC calls my name, and I had nothing.

I went on stage and pleaded for the miscreant who took my trunk/suitcase to return it. No one did anything. I said, well, when I was a Boy Scout, I lived by the motto we were morally upright, and whoever did this was not abiding by that standard. Still nothing.

I said, "Well, I'm sorry, I will not be performing tonight. Thanks for inviting me." And I left the stage. About 20 minutes later, someone found my trunk stashed in a janitor's closet. I picked it up, and I left.

As a Boy Scout myself for years, I would never have thought it would be the only show where I had to cancel. Never have I ever had my props moved and hidden from me. And frankly, I was doing that show for free to give back to an organization that had taught me so much when I was a member. Evidently, not everyone got the same message from being a Boy Scout that I got. Too sad.

I am a criminal litigator. My clowning experience has come in handy when cross-examining witnesses recalcitrant in answering questions from the defense. But with a bit of clown cajoling, I can finagle a change of heart and get what I need from them.

Email: *MFWillimann@mfwlawoffice.com*

Chapter 30
Regina 'ChaCha' Wollrabe

Celebration and Closure

I'm always grateful when I have a rewarding event full of laughter and happy kids with happy parents because they had such a positive time. I love it when kids say, "You're silly, you funny clown!" I also love it when I've helped distract people from their rough times or loss or ease the pain of awkwardness in any situation.

I recall a party where I performed a few years ago. This party was tough to do, but so important. It was one of those days I was fulfilling the clown prayer on the back of my Clowns of America International membership card.

I received a call from a grandmother who chose to hire a clown to celebrate the daddy of her two granddaughters. Everything was routine for booking this party until I learned their daddy had died two months prior. The little girls and their mom were undergoing a rough time anticipating it was his birthday soon. I had never done a party like this before.

Before the party, I prayed, "Lord please support me do my best and help these little girls laugh and have fun." Friends and children packed the house. Balloons were here and there, and a banner graced the fireplace with the dad's name. The magic words were "Happy Birthday, David!" When we sang happy birthday to him the girls blew out daddy's candles on the cake.

We went outside to release balloons to the heavens and yelled as loud as we could, "Happy Birthday, Daddy, we love you!" We watched the balloons disappear into the sky. It was hard to fight back the tears.

I stayed after the party. Guests left, and I sat on the steps talking with the girls about the things that interest them. As I left that night, the tearful mom said, "This is the first time my girls have laughed and had fun since their daddy died. Thank you for making tonight so special for them." We hugged for a long time, I felt so honored to have had that experience, and on the drive home I cried.

It's interesting that in clowning we can feel the pain of failure. However, the pain that comes from the sadness we hold while we help a family or person escape their grief even for a moment, cannot be explained except through shedding a few tears ourselves.

Thank you, Lord, for giving us the opportunities to create healing laughter for those who bear such pain.

Regina Wollrabe was born and raised in Portland, Oregon. Winning the first place at a high school state theatre competition in mime was the catalyst to a lifelong fascination with performing and teaching.

She performed in a traveling mime troupe in 1985–87 and became a professional clown and member of Clowns of America International (COAI) in 1991, while raising four boys who clowned alongside her.

Appointed the COAI Jr. Joey Chair in 2012, ChaCha was Best in Clown at the Convention in 2013 and Clown of the Year in 2016. Regina is the Director of Jr. Joeys for COAI.

Website: *http://chachatheclown.com*

Chapter 31
Heather 'Pockets' Wuersching

Pockets Almost Never Was

My introduction to clowning was a little unsettling, to say the least.

Back in 2007, with my daughters grown up, I decided I wanted to do some volunteering to give back to my community. I heard about a group that called themselves Caring Clowns. I thought "That could be interesting." I went along to a meeting and joined up.

With very little information, let alone instruction, I choose Pockets for a clown name. I put together a costume with lots of pockets, decided on a clown face I could manage and I put my name down to clown at a hospital.

My first day, only Twaddles was there to be my guide. Little did we realize that this was the beginning of a wonderful adventure. I was excited and really looked forward to the experience, but we arrived at the reception desk only to be told, "Sorry, the hospital was put in lock down an hour ago. There is a virus outbreak, so no clowns today." I was somewhat deflated.

Twaddles suggested we go have a coffee and have a chat about clowning, and such. We went to a coffee shop, and I had my first lesson in balloon twisting as well as becoming a little more relaxed about interacting with strangers while dressed as a clown. Although it was nothing like the day I had expected, it was not a complete waste of time.

The next outing was to another hospital. This time there were Twaddles and another male clown. Again, I was excited and couldn't wait to get into the silly stuff.

We signed in at reception, made it to the nurses' station and was told, "Start in room 3. There is a six-year-old girl in there dying from cancer, she hasn't got long. Her parents are with her, and they could do with a distraction."

"What? Is she serious?" I almost quit right then. My heart was in my boots, and my brain was exploding. I could not believe we were being asked to go into that room and be clowns while a child dies. Being a mother,

I felt that there was no way I could do it. I guess I did not want to make a scene, so with great trepidation, I traipsed along behind the two men and we entered the room.

I don't remember too clearly, because my mind was in complete turmoil, but the child was awake and the clowns spoke softly to her.

I think we sang a quiet lullaby, talked a little with the parents, made a couple of balloon animals, and we made our exit.

We were just out the door when the mother came out, threw her arms around me and with tears running down her face, said to the three of us "Thank you so much for doing that.

It gave us something else to think about for a few minutes, and we needed that."

The lights came on in my brain, my spirit soared as I realized that Yes! That is what caring clowning is about, and I have lived for it since that day.

I started clowning in 2007 with a local Group in Queensland, Australia. I regularly took part in more than four visits a month to patients in hospitals and residents in aged-care facilities.

In 2010, trying to develop my clown skills, I attended the Red Skelton Clown School with fellow clown Twaddles. It was conducted at the University of Vincennes in Indiana. We were invited back to Vincennes in 2013 to teach the junior clown students at the Red Skelton Junior Joey School. I thoroughly embraced the experience.

In 2014 I was appointed an Ambassador to Clowns of American International (COAI) and started attending COAI Conventions in Erie, Pennsylvania, and Las Vegas, Nevada. In 2017 Pockets joined forces with Twaddles for a new clown adventure.

Email: *wuersching61@dodo.com.au*

Chapter 32
Leslie Ann 'Flower' Akin

Acting on a Prompting

 During the late '70s, the local hospital where I lived in Maryland allowed me carte blanche to visit patients whenever I was in clown makeup.

This option was handy because I could perform for a few parties, then scoot over to the hospital for a few rounds. The staff even invited my character, Dokter Popcorn, into the emergency room to distract patients while they waited. Once the real doctor arrived, I skedaddled.

On one of my Saturday after-show rounds in an adult wing, something unusual happened—at least for a hospital visit. The patient, Gregg, was in his late 30s. Family members were visiting, and they squealed with gleeful delight as I entered. This was a lively bunch.

Since there was no one in the next bed, we could play full-tilt without annoying another patient. It didn't take much to engage these fine folks in light-hearted bantering. We carried on for ten minutes. As I left, they applauded and cheered.

On the following Tuesday, I had plans for the day. However, I could not shake the compelling instinct I should get into makeup and go visiting at the hospital. I wondered why, but because this was a powerful prompting that would not pass, I did just that.

I took a detour to a toy store and purchased a small toy doctor's bag. Then off to the hospital and made rounds as Dokter Popcorn. After visiting ten people, I wondered if Gregg was still here. I checked that room, and there he was, alone and sitting upright, panicked and sweating profusely. I only took a few steps into the room and stopped.

Gregg shouted, "Dokter Popcorn, I *needed* to see you! I'm going into surgery in a few minutes!" My heart skipped a beat, I'm sure. This moment was far from the merriment and mirth that occurred only days prior with Gregg and his family. I reached into the prop bag hanging off my shoulder, grabbed my eighteen-inch plastic scissors, held them high in the air, exclaiming, "It's okay, I'm assisting!"

Gregg's much-needed burst of spontaneous laughter fueled my nervous energy. I squashed Gregg's fears for the moment; now I had to keep the momentum up.

I placed my brand-new toy doctor's bag on Gregg's rolling table, saying, "Let's see what we have in here. Oh, look, I have glasses." I placed the silly child-sized plastic specs over my clown nose.

Gregg was more than amused, giggling like a little girl. Next came the stethoscope, placed on his wrist, and after doctor-like grumbles, I affirmed, "Yes, you take a licking and keep on ticking." Gregg was wildly amused. Next, I looked for another toy I expected to be inside the bag—but wasn't.

Hands on my hips and patting my big floppy foot impatiently on the linoleum floor, with flailing arms I quipped, "Seven-fifty for this thing and there's no—" I could not think of the word. I mimed a doctor giving someone a shot.

Gregg doubled over laughing at my clown-hissy-fit. He tried to say the word, but all that came out was "Saaaahh—" and more giggling.

The more I played on this bit, "Seven-fifty for this and there's no—" the more Gregg laughed. I kept tapping my foot in clown-like disgust with spirit and silliness.

Gregg finally got the word out, "Saaah-ringe!" I replied, "Yes, that's it! Syringe!" I broke character, bending over laughing with Gregg. That time, breaking character worked.

Our looney laugh-fest became the real world again when orderlies appeared, placing Gregg on the gurney to head into surgery.

Gregg didn't want me to leave him, so I took the long walk beside him as far as they allowed me, holding his hand. I told him I'd be with him in spirit. He squeezed my hand. The double doors swung closed in front of me. I realized why getting to the hospital fell so hard on my heart that day.

The strangest part of this experience is that I had never had this kind of overwhelming prompting before. In my years of clowning, I had never handled something so sensitive, and if I had known what I was to walk into that day, I may have done so with more concern. Instead, I was in the room when I realized the seriousness and urgency of Gregg's situation. I wasn't prepared, yet I was—because I did it. I believe it was by the grace of God.

When I think of how perfect the timing was—that I responded to the prompting, stopped for a toy, visited other patients, and finally considered that Gregg might still be there—I know there is a divine order that allowed for everything to align.

I wondered if God was checking his Timex, tapping his foot, saying, "Leslie Ann, get your red nose in your red Dodge Dart Swinger and get to the hospital now. Stop wondering. Just do it!"

I've learned to listen carefully for such promptings.

Leslie Ann Akin is the publisher of this book and the author of A Fool's Guide to Clowning *with Global Touch Press. Leslie Ann is the publisher of* Jest for Clowns, *a digital magazine delivered to clowns worldwide six times a year.*

Leslie Ann Akin, also known as "Flower T. Clown," appeared under the Big Top with Clyde Beatty-Cole Bros., Hoxie Bros., and Great American Circuses and was featured on the nationally syndicated television show PM Magazine. *In addition to Leslie's busy performance schedule, she was a long-time featured columnist for* The Laugh Makers *magazine, a publication for family-style entertainers.*

Leslie Ann was the recipient of the coveted Emmett (Kelly Sr.) Award for her contributions to the circus and clowning. Her vast performing experience encompassed charities, embassies, fairs, and even twice at the White House. Leslie performed in Washington, D.C., for many years.

After relocating to the San Francisco Bay area, she teamed up with Steve Dawson and Steve Rancatore to form Three Ring Enterprises, a circus-arts performing and lecturing team dedicated to providing wholesome family entertainment.

After a long and successful career in clowning, Leslie Ann still has a love and passion for sharing her experiences and mentoring new clowns.

Leslie Ann is a strategic brand specialist and owns LeslieTheBrandBoss.com in Lake Oswego, Oregon.

Website: *http://LeslieTheBrandBoss.com*
Publication: *https://www.JestForClowns.com*
Facebook: *https://www.facebook.com/groups/ AFoolsGuideToClowning*

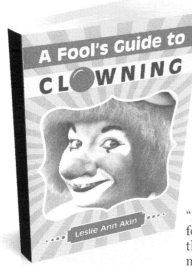

CHAPTERS

01. Wacky One-Liners
02. Ring-A-Ding-Ding
03. Tiny Knee-slappers
04. Colossal Knee-slappers
05. Whopping Warm-ups
06. Nitty-Gritty of Birthday Parties
07. Mirthdays are for Laughing
08. Hanky Panky, Where's My Hanky?
09. Mr. Party Animal
10. Comedy Magic with Peanuts
11. Vanilla the Wondiferous Wonder Bunny
12. Picnics with Pizazz
13. Clowns Taste Funny
14. Would You Like a Side of Clown with That Pizza?
15. Anatomy of a Hospital Clown
16. Clown Control at The White House
17. The Sole of a Clown
18. Tune-up Time for Touring
19. A Spectacle of Big Top Escapades
20. Circus Slanguage
21. Clown Resources
22. BONUS: The Performer's Guide to Smart Business

BE R
WEB CONTENT

Jan Bear

wordsmith

book
designer

web
manager

Jan@
BearWebContent.com

  503.807.4611

Made in the USA
Monee, IL
11 April 2021